The Source of Wealth

F. Patrick Cunnane

Table of Contents

Life as a Pension Consultant

The happy couple about to retire walks into my temporary on-site office which is provided by the host corporation. Usually it's the office of someone who is on vacation. I set up shop with several chairs, a laptop with charts and graphs, a few handouts, and my HP calculator to estimate the potential future value of pensioners' assets. Everyone in the company will stop in for a brief review to see if their long-term savings are on target. "How many years to retirement?" "How much in the 401(k) presently?" "How much can you save?" "Save more," "You're OK," "Wow, that is a very good balance, you are in great shape."

Management typically encourages employees to bring their spouses to meet with me, if possible, and occasionally I see a couple, as opposed to just individual employees. Hence the happy couple. I can see they are happy. Reading faces is a standard skill of most consultants. Besides, I have everyone's account balances, which I review before they walk through the door. I know they are happy because they are retiring in what appears to be good health and ample assets in the 401(k)/profit sharing accounts. They beam while telling me about their plans. The Winnebego for the out-west-somewhere trip of a lifetime, visiting the kids in Arizona, his fishing cabin and her time to take it easy and reflect. A good time. Proud they earned it. They don't need my advice; they are showing off. I am happy for them. Sincerely happy because they are the few: the successful ones.

Then, with far too much frequency, the couple with no or little assets walks in. I don't want to read their faces. They are sad, they have been fighting; I can see they have been married forty years, and they love each other. He is a kind, uneducated gentleman. Honest with big-knuckled broken hands; hands that have done many a day's work. Her eyes are red. I know she has been crying. Deep down they know this meeting is a waste of time, but they show up anyway. They are hoping I have some financial whiz-kid trick that can save them.

I do not have any tricks. They must think I lack sympathy because I act somewhat indifferently toward them. Cold and emotionless in a matter-of-fact fashion; the way an experienced physician breaks the bad news to the terminally ill or to anxious loved ones in the hospital waiting room. The bearer of redundant bad news: no empathy, no emotion and not the slightest hint of sorrow. I say, "You don't have enough to retire on." The wife will half look at me and glance at her husband of many years and softly say, with a throat tightened by worry, "Social security is not enough." He will hang his head in a prayerful pose and say, "Social security is not enough." I chime in, "Social security is not enough." God, if I hear, "Social security is not enough" one more time I . . .

I am sick of seeing sad faces. What bothers me is the sad faces I see are 100 percent curable. It is possible to create long-term savings where all the sad faces are eliminated.

The Law of the Land

Congress has told all businesses to operate their profit sharing and 401(k) plans under an employee-directed system. That means you, the employee, are responsible to manage the assets in your profit sharing and/or 401(k) plan. The corporation will supply the system under which the assets (money) will be deposited, but it is up to each individual to decide how to manage a multinational portfolio of stocks, bonds and cash.

The problem is, most people are not educated in the fine art of asset management. The goal is simple. The investor must retire wealthy. How does the investor go from non-wealthy to wealthy? The good news is it takes very little money to become wealthy. The bad news is the investor must understand how the process functions to succeed. Put money into the 401(k) plan. Then something happens to the money and wealth comes out upon retirement. What happens to the money to make it change from a small amount of money to enough wealth to retire on?

This book is designed to show the average corporate employee, who does not have a financial background, how the process of wealth creation functions. The process of economics that turns the currency in our pockets into wealth must be learned for an employee to have enough assets to retire.

To manage a self-directed 401(k) and/or profit sharing plan, the employee must learn a set of economic principals.

The successful investor must understand how the economy creates wealth if he wants to accumulate it. The process of understanding wealth accumulation is as follows:

1. Money or currency (dollar bills and coins) is only a measurement device.
2. Currency is not an investment.
3. All wealth is derived from corporate profits.
4. All investment returns are actually corporate profit returns.
5. To accumulate wealth, then, is to accumulate corporate profits.

By reviewing the business of a coal-mining corporation, it is easy to follow the step-by-step process of how wealth is created. The process of wealth creation begins with the business activity of the corporation. A coal mine produces coal: its product is coal. The activity of the coal mine is coal production. The mine must produce enough coal to pay for the internal expenses of the mining activity. Therefore, Step One of the creation of wealth is business activity.

In addition to producing enough coal to pay for the internal expense of the mine, there must also be a surplus of coal production which is above the production necessary to operate the mine. The surplus generated is Step Two in the creation of wealth. The extra coal produced above the internal operating needs of the mine is called a profit. The profit is used to pay taxes, upgrade equipment, research more efficient production methods, pay workers' benefits, buy more coal-rich deposits, and pay the lenders and owners a return on their use of resources.

The product of the mining corporation is coal, and although coal provides many necessary benefits to society, it cannot be used in its natural state to fulfill the many liabilities of the corporation. The corporation must have the coal measured and transformed into a corresponding amount of a common median of exchange. The workers cannot use coal to buy food, clothing, and shelter. The corporation cannot give coal to the government to meet its tax liability. In the United States of America the common median of exchange is the dollar. The coal must be measured, and based on the results of the measurement, then be exchanged for dollars. So much coal is worth so many dollars. This process of measuring the coal and transforming it into dollars is called measurementism and is Step Three in the creation of wealth.

For simplicity, suppose a pound of coal corresponds to one dollar. If the coal mine produced a million pounds of coal per year then the mining corporation would generate a million dollars per year. The corporation would use part of the million dollars to pay the internal costs of production and the remaining dollars, which are the profit, would be used to pay for all the additional obligations. To pay for the additional obligations, the corporation must be able to dig coal, pay for digging, and then have a lot of dollars left over. The leftover dollars are the profit.

Before the profit which the owners and workers created can be enjoyed, approximately half of it must be given to the government in the form of corporate taxes. This is Step Four in the flow of wealth through society, and it affects the return on investment. As a dollar of profit is created by the mine, the dollar is reduced to $0.50 by the government before any of the people who created the profit can partake of it.

Of the remaining $0.50, half of it, or $0.25, is given to the government in the form of individual income taxes. Of the original dollar created by the mine, only $0.25 remains to pay the people who created the profit. This is Step Five. The $0.25 is then further pinched by local officials to the point where approximately $0.20 remains for the producers to live off of. This is Step Six.

Finally, the remaining $0.20 of the profit created by the mining corporation is used to pay for daily living expenses of those who created it and a portion of the $0.20, approximately one penny, is returned to the corporation as an investment. This $0.01, or one percent of the original dollar created, is all that remains of the initial profit which the mine created. The only investment choice available for the investor is to put the $0.01 of savings back into the corporation. Investing the penny back into the corporation is the final step in the creation of wealth.

The following describes the creation of wealth.

Step 1:

BUSINESS
ACTIVITY

Producing the
Product

From corporate business activity, the corporation generates value from its product that exceeds the internal needs of the corporation. The value in excess of its internal needs is profit.

Step 2:

PROFIT IS
CREATED FROM
CORPORATE
ACTIVITY

and profit is
a surplus

All wealth comes from
corporate profits.

Initially, profits are in terms of the product, whatever the product is (in the previous example it is coal, but it could be anything). The profit in

Step 2 is in terms of a product. The product must be transformed into currency or dollars. Step 3 is transforming corporate profits into dollars by measurementism.

Step 3:

Corporate product is transferred into dollars through measurementism. The dollars are used to meet corporate obligations. The first obligation of the corporation is to give approximately half of the corporate profits to the government through corporate tax.

Step 3:

Step 4:

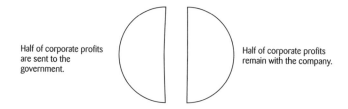

Of the original dollars of corporate profit created by the corporation, only $0.50 remains after corporate taxes are paid.

The remaining $0.50 is taxed again through individual income tax. The government again takes half of the $0.50 making it $0.25. Step 5 is the individual income tax.

Step 5:

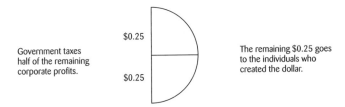

$0.25

Government taxes
half of the remaining
corporate profits.

The remaining $0.25 goes
to the individuals who
created the dollar.

$0.25

Of the initial dollar of wealth created by the corporation, $0.75 or more is taken by the government and $0.25 goes to the citizens who created the wealth.

Still more government tax is taken from corporate profits and the individuals who earned the profits in the form of local and state sales tax, goods tax and real estate tax. These mark-ups by the government further shrink the individual's share of corporate profits to about $0.20 on the dollar.

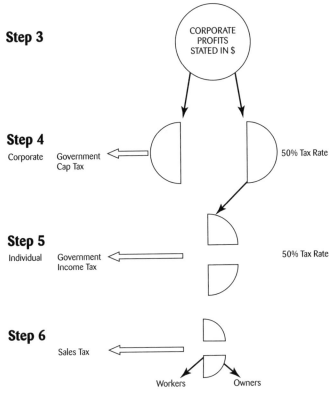

Step 3

CORPORATE
PROFITS
STATED IN $

Step 4

Corporate   Government
Cap Tax

50% Tax Rate

Step 5

Individual   Government
Income Tax

50% Tax Rate

Step 6

Sales Tax

Workers   Owners

1 x .5 x .5 x .8 = $0.20

The worker/owner now has $0.25 of every dollar she/he created and government has $0.75 of every dollar created from corporate activity. The worker/owner only has one investment choice with her savings: to invest in business activity. Local officials further reduce the $0.25 to $0.20 through state and local taxes.

Step 1

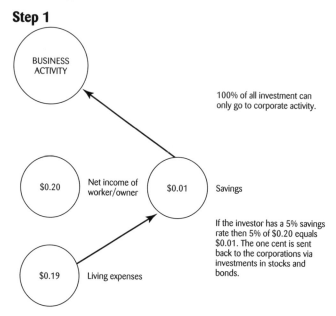

There are only two investment choices:

1) Buying ownership in corporate activity
2) Lending currency to corporate activity

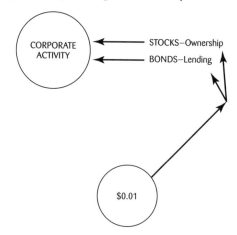

The stockholder is the owner of corporate activity and its resulting profits. The stockholder receives 100 percent of the corporate profits relative to the percentage of ownership. If a corporation generates profit at a rate of 10 percent per year then the stockholder in turn will earn similar gains.

The bondholder is not an owner and therefore is not entitled to receive the rate of growth of the corporation. As a lender, the bondholder receives a fixed rate of return, typically half the rate of average corporate profits. If the rate of growth of corporate profits is 10 percent then the bondholder will earn a rate of return approximately half of 10 percent, or 5 percent on average.

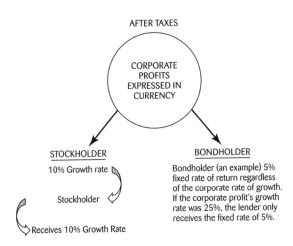

The owners of corporate activity and the resulting profits must grow in aggregate at twice the lending rate over time. Therefore the rate of return the owners will receive is twice that of bonds. Any individual can choose whether she wants to lend currency to corporate activity or become an owner in corporate activity. Owners become owners by purchasing shares of stock and lenders become lenders by purchasing bonds.

The economy begins at Step 1, corporate activity. For the investor to become richer the investor must focus on Step 1. What makes the workers and owners richer? Only one event can make society richer and that is increasing corporate profits. A country with the highest corporate profits per individual is the richest country per individual (highest per capita income) or, to put it another way, a country with the highest amount of corporate profits would then be the richest country (largest Gross Domestic Product) on earth.

The United States is the richest country in the world because it has more corporate profits than any other country. If all U.S. corporations relocated to country X then country X would be the richest country. The purple mountains are fun to look upon, but it is the corporate profits that are the wealth.

Therefore, the successful investor pursues corporate profits. The more corporate profits an individual owns, the richer he is. The pursuit of wealth over a lifetime is the pursuit of corporate profits over a lifetime.

A police officer just saved a life at the risk of his own, the marine just saved the country, a fire fighter just saved a child from a fire. We all are lucky to have them. But without corporate profits they would not exist. In war our tank blew up the enemy tank. Our tank is better because we are richer, we have more corporate profits so we can afford to build a better weapon.

Where does the money come from to pay those who do not create to corporate profits—the teachers, the mayors, county clerks, congressional representatives, fire fighters, police officers, soldiers, sailors, airmen, marines, social workers, welfare recipients, social security recipients, and so on.

Civil servants are paid from the corporate activity of the steel worker, bricklayer, carpenter, pipe fitter, truck driver, corporate lawyer, manager, engineer, corporate president, corporate vice president, ship worker, and so on.

When a police officer receives her paycheck, 100 percent of the money represented in the check is courtesy of Microsoft, Ford Motor Company, GM, GE, WalMart, Proctor and Gamble—the corporate profits of all U.S. businesses. The money came from corporate profits. Somebody's sweat, work, toil, fear of being fired, fear of a bad decision, and/or sleepless nights are a part of these profits. The money comes from corporate profits, not the government. The government does not have any money. The government gets its money from taking a slice—a big slice—from corporate profits.

When a social security recipient receives his check, 100 percent of the money represented in the check came from corporate profits, not the government.

That which reduces corporate profits hurts us all. If a Social Security recipient would like to continue to receive her check, she better make certain she protects the source of the money, which is corporate activity and its resulting profits. No profits equals no money equals no checks.

Managing a 401(k) and/or a profit sharing plan is managing corporate profits.

Introduction to the Planet Corn and the Hunting Village

To enable the investor to easily differentiate between currency (money) and real wealth (corporate profits), the following imaginary societies are created.

First, Planet Corn is a world 100 percent dependent upon agriculture. It is a world with only a single commodity, corn, from which all things are made and all needs are met. The second world—Hunting Village—is a pre-industrial hunting society whose citizens survive exclusively on deer meat and deer by-products. The metaphor of the two single commodity worlds will allow the reader to avoid the mathematics of the economists, but still gain an understanding of how an economy offers its citizens the opportunity to become wealthy.

These two single commodity worlds will filter out the millions of possible events in our present society, making it easier to understand the financial process based on just one economic event. The source of wealth in a single commodity world is the commodity or the process by which the commodity is integrated into the economy. With only one commodity from which all things are made, the process and the commodity are one in the same, making it easy to understand the process. Understanding the source of wealth in a modern economy is possible by focusing on the process and filtering out the millions of products, services, and raw materials.

The Planet Corn

The Planet Corn is a world where only a single plant exists; there are no animals, no valuable minerals, and all manufactured goods are made exclusively from the corn plant. Corn meets all survival needs. The people of Planet Corn obtain 100 percent of their daily nutrition from corn, they drink corn juice, manufacture all finished goods from corn, and live in houses made of corn. Planet Corn's human population is very similar to the population on Earth except Planet Corn has only a single commodity from which all things are made: corn. This world is not too different from living on a corn farm in Kentucky where a corn farmer eats corn bread for dinner, drinks moonshine for entertainment, and has grits for breakfast.

How do the people of Planet Corn transact business to meet their daily needs? If a woman wanted to buy a shovel, which is manufactured exclusively from the corn plant, from the hardware store, what form of payment would she use? The seller would establish a price, such as ten pounds of corn. The buyer must then pay ten pounds of corn to the seller in exchange for the shovel. The buyer could carry ten pounds of real corn to the hardware store for the exchange, which would force the buyer to lug around baskets of corn to pay for everyday needs. If someone wanted to purchase a new house, it would be extremely impractical to pay the seller in actual corn. The price of a new house on Planet Corn could be ten tons of corn, a truckload. What would the seller do with a truckload of corn? It would be impossible to store, transport, or put into a safety deposit box.

The government of Planet Corn needs to establish an arbitrary unit of paper money, which represents value, or a corresponding amount of corn. The unit of currency could be based on weight. One corn dollar would be worth one pound of actual corn, a ten-corn dollar bill would be worth ten pounds of corn and so on. This would enable the purchasers of larger, more expensive products to pay with paper currency, which would represent large amounts of actual corn. If a four-bedroom house costs twenty tons of corn then the buyer would give the seller twenty one-ton-corn bills. The buyer of the shovel, which is worth ten real pounds of corn, would pay the hardware store with a ten-pound-corn bill rather then deliver the actual ten pounds of corn.

On a planet-wide basis there are millions and millions of tons of corn grown annually from which all products are made. The people of Planet Corn are making millions of transactions every day and it would be impossible to deliver the actual corn for each transaction. It would be impossible for a citizen of Planet Corn to carry enough corn on her person to make all possible transactions. Travel would be impossible, as the traveler would have to carry tons of corn with him wherever he went. Suppose the corn became lost or stolen: what would a stranded traveler do?

The government of Planet Corn has the authority to print the official corn bills to use for currency. Once the value of the currency is established, such as one corn bill equals one pound of corn, then the number of bills printed must correspond to the actual pounds of corn in existence. The corn bills printed must be relative to corn production. If one million pounds of corn is produced, then the government can only print one million one-pound-corn bills. The one million pounds of actual corn are measured; the measurement is used to determine the amount of currency printed. This process of measuring production and printing currency to match the value of production is called measurementism.

By only printing the number of corn bills that correspond to the actual corn production, the shopkeepers can be assured the corn bill received for goods and services sold are actually worth a corresponding amount of corn. That is, if a shopkeeper receives a ten-pound-corn bill, he can be assured the bill is actually worth a real ten pounds of corn. This way the shopkeeper can properly account for the difference between the cost of production and retail price. Therefore, as long as the government prints the exact number of corn bills directly corresponding to the weight of actual production, then the price of goods and services should remain relatively constant over time. That is, as long as the printing of corn bills equals actual corn production, then the price of a shovel should remain ten corn dollars year to year (assuming supply and demand are normal). Supply and demand should remain fairly constant from year to year because there is only one commodity on Planet Corn.

What then is the most likely catalyst to cause an increase in the price of corn and/or goods and services? If the government decides, for whatever reason, to print more corn bills then there is actual corn production to justify, the price of all goods and services will increase. If the government prints 10 percent more bills than there is production, then the shovel at the hardware store, which is actually worth ten pounds of corn, will still be worth ten pounds of corn, but it will take eleven corn bills to buy it. The shovel did not change in value: it took the resources of ten pounds of corn to produce it and put it on the shelf of the store. What has changed is the value of the money.

For example, if one million pounds of corn were produced, then the government should print one million one-pound-corn bills. If the politicians made promises to the people in order to buy votes, and the cost of the promise exceeds the actual production of corn by 10 percent, then the government must print 10 percent more bills, or 10 percent times one million which equals one million one hundred thousand. There are now one hundred thousand more bills in circulation then there should be, which is 10 percent more. This means a one-pound-corn bill is not worth one pound of actual corn anymore. It now takes a one-pound-corn bill and ten corn cents to equal an actual pound of real corn. It now takes eleven corn bills to equal ten real pounds of corn.

The shovel is worth ten real pounds of corn, but the buyer must now pay eleven one-pound-bills to buy it. It is not the shovel that has changed in value. Shovels cannot change in value. If it takes ten pounds of resources to produce the shovel then the shovel is actually worth ten real pounds of corn. It is the currency that has changed in value and it now takes more currency to equal one pound of actual corn. The shovel is more expensive for no other reason then a politician promising to spend more money then actual production could justify, and to meet the promise, the politician overprinted the supply of money. The shopkeeper is not a bad person for raising the price. In actuality the price of the shovel stayed the same, it was the value of the money which changed, not the product. The citizen is forced to pay more for the shovel by the politician who caused the overprinting of the currency. It is the politician's fault.

The overprinting of money is such a common practice it has been given a term: inflation. Inflation is simply when the government prints more currency then there is production to justify. Inflation has been a common practice of the government over the past two hundred years of U.S. history and there have been only a few years when inflation did not occur.

Some inflation is justifiable, as the overprinting of money is necessary to allow for growth and innovation. If a farmer on Planet Corn invented a new production process which increased corn output then there must be enough currency in existence to finance (allow the inventor to borrow money) the invention and put it into practice. The borrowed currency is in excess of what the economy can justify. That is, Planet Corn can only generate so much money per year and the money needed to put the new invention into practice is in excess of what justifiably can be printed. The use of excess currency causes inflation, but it is essential to the implementation of the new invention. As slight overprinting is necessary to allow for growth, the resulting inflation has then become a historical constant and it is safe to assume inflation will continue into the future. Consistent ongoing inflation will constantly reduce the value of the currency. This is why the ten-corn-dollar shovel experiences a price increase to eleven corn dollars. The currency is over printed, creating a situation where more currency is needed in order to buy goods and services year to year.

In addition to inflation, the citizens of Planet Corn suffer another setback due to taxes. On Planet Corn the government is particularly ruthless, virtually enslaving the population by demanding each citizen work for free for nine to ten months per year, leaving the overburdened workers with only 20 to 30 percent of their income.

The tax system on Planet Corn taxes both the actual farming operations, which grow the corn, as well as the income of the people who work on the farm. The local district, called a corn state, also taxes the income and purchases of the corn workers.

If a farmer can grow a thousand pounds of corn per week, it creates a thousand pounds of wealth for the citizens of Planet Corn to enjoy. The tax system deprives the citizens of the thousand pounds of wealth (one thousand one-pound-corn bills would be generated) because the thousand pounds is taxed at 50 percent (the standard corporate rate), leaving only 50 percent remaining. The remaining five hundred pounds of corn is sent into the economic system instead of the thousand pounds. The result is, the ten-dollar-corn shovel should have cost five dollars, but the corn citizen is forced to pay ten dollars, which is a 100 percent increase in price. The 100 percent increase in price is a direct result of the producing farm being taxed at 50 percent (the corporate rate). If there was no corporate tax, then the shovel would only cost five corn pounds instead of ten corn pounds. Products must be sold at a 100 percent markup to recover the 50 percent corporate tax rate.

The difference of only five dollars on a shovel does not seem overburdensome until larger, more expensive items are considered. A house on Planet Corn which is on the market for 100,000 corn bills would only cost 50,000 if there were no corporate tax. The corn citizens lose 50,000 for no other reason than the producing farm was taxed. The 50,000 corn bill savings would enable the homebuyer to purchase a yacht, small airplane or vacation cabin, build a swimming pool, and/or buy a second car. The government of Planet Corn tells the people that the mean old producing farm is greedy and deserves to be taxed and the Corn citizens who suffer from brain damage due to a purely starch diet believe it. How is paying 100 percent more for everything a good idea?

In addition to taxing the farming operation which produces the corn that people need to survive, the government also taxes the income of the average person who works growing the corn approximately 50 percent. The worker who started out with a thousand corn bills per week is reduced to five hundred from corporate taxation. The income tax reduces it by 50 percent again, taking the original thousand pounds to 250 pounds. The total tax between corporate and income tax leaves the worker with 250 pounds of spending power from her thousand pounds of earned labor. If there was no tax at all then the worker could buy four times as much.

If the average worker could afford a 100,000-corn-bill house after taxes, then they could also afford four times as much before taxes, such as a 100,000-corn-bill vacation home, plus a small yacht, a third vacation home, and a luxury car to drive around. The best way to understand a four-fold increase in spending power is to imagine owning a house, a vacation home, a boat, and a fine car, then having the government take away the vacation home, boat, and car. Ask yourself if the loss of your lifestyle due to excessive government spending is a good deal.

It is a good thing Planet Corn is a make-believe world because the following tax rule is so far outside rational reasoning it could only occur in a make-believe society. The rule on Planet Corn is to tax the smart people more then the average worker. For instance, the doctor who just saved your life or your child's life loses five times his purchasing power. That is, those who earn more suffer more under the tax system. The worker has 75 percent of the money taken by the government while the average doctor has 80 percent of his earnings taken.

This planet has created two major problems for the investor: inflation and taxes. Inflation, or the overprinting of money, constantly reduces the value of money, which causes the problem of constant rising prices for all goods and services. This problem with printed money is not new. Prior to modern day currency, most of the world used precious metal such as gold and silver to mint coins. This made it so the government could not overprint gold because gold has a finite supply. The problem with using gold or any precious metal is that the precious metal has nothing to do with production. If a cure for cancer was discovered on Planet Corn some extra money would need to be printed to create the drug factory to produce the cure. If there was not enough gold, then the cancer cure could not be implemented. The gold standard makes growth and invention very slow in coming to market. The United States abandoned the precious metal system in the 1970s.

Money is not wealth. Production is wealth. Around the time of the American Civil War, accumulating confederate money was a mistake because the South lost and the paper money had no value. A tobacco farm was worth as much before the war as it was after because the farm produced something of value, whereas money is only used as a medium of exchange.

Money is the least efficient asset to accumulate because it constantly decreases in value through inflation. As she develops an investment strategy, the investor is faced with constant inflation and taxes, which push the value of money backwards.

Most citizens of Planet Corn have two long-term savings methods to help them accumulate enough wealth to be able to live comfortably during retirement. One system is operated by the government of Planet Corn and the other system is operated by the owner of the farming operation, which is the private sector. The government-operated savings program is called Social Security and the private sector savings plan is typically profit sharing and a 401(k) plan.

The government savings program, Social Security, is a system into which every citizen is forced to deposit part of their income, about 7 percent of his or her gross earnings, into a retirement plan. The farming business (employer) is also required to deposit an additional 7 percent of gross earnings on the employee's behalf. For the average Planet Corn person who worked forty-five years earning 35,000 corn bills per year, the payment at retirement should be 40,000 corn bills per month plus a payment of 4.5 million corn bills to family members in case of an unexpected death early into retirement.

The problem is, the government on Planet Corn steals 97 percent of the monthly payment, reducing it to approximately 1000 corn bills per month in lieu of 40,000 corn bills and steals 100 percent of the payment for premature death. The money saved by the average worker should be 4 to 5 million corn bills, but the Social Security saver only gets 100,000 corn bills or less—or 3 to 5 percent of what they are entitled to, or 3 to 5 corn cents on the dollar. Plus the Social Security saver forfeits 100 percent of his 4 to 5 million corn bills if he dies shortly after retiring. All of the stolen money goes to the politicians in government specifically to make their lives more comfortable while the average worker is rendered miserable. The politician naturally rejects the idea of reforming Social Security because she would lose all the stolen money. The people do not know a theft has occurred because the people do not know how the financial system operates. Ignorance on Planet Corn is rampant.

As if stealing 97 percent of a retiree's money is not enough, the government also taxes the remaining 1000 corn bills per month as income. The politician's retirement plan pays 20,000 corn bills per month.

On Planet Corn a corporate savings plan is a profit-sharing plan sponsored by the producing farm for the benefit of the employees. A portion of corporate profits are deposited into a real account which the employee owns. A 401(k) uses a similar type of savings account except the employee can deposit a small percentage of his earnings into his account in addition to the corporate deposit.

To contrast the efficiency of the government and corporate retirement plans, compare the corn bill amounts of deposits necessary to generate 1000 corn bills per month for the retiree. The corporate-sponsored plan can generate 1000 corn bills per month from a 100-corn-bill annual deposit over a worker's lifetime when the government-operated plan requires a deposit fifty times larger to accomplish the same result. Obviously the government-run system is an extreme waste of resources. The corporate system can generate enough retirement income to better or equal the employee's income during her working years. The Social Security system saves much more money using more resources and completely fails to meet the retiree's needs simply because the government steals 97 percent of the money.

The best strategy for long-term savings is to invest in the corporate plan and not attempt to depend on the government-run plan (Social Security).

The Planet Forest

The goal is to accumulate wealth over a lifetime. The source of wealth is a very simple concept when it is explained in the context of a single commodity world. Imagine Planet Forest. It is a world covered in forest, inhabited by preindustrial villagers, where there are no edible plants and the only source of food is the sole animal, which is deer. The only source of food is deer meat, the only source of clothing is deer skin and 100 percent of all the villagers' needs (that is, food, clothing, and shelter) are met by deer or deer by-products.

Deer are fast and elusive and the villagers are limited by technology to hunting with only spears. A single hunter is incapable of producing enough deer to support himself and his family. The only way the villagers can survive is to organize a hunting party and hunt as a group. Then by surrounding the deer and creating an ever-smaller circle the hunters give the deer no choice but to eventually run head on into an awaiting spear.

The successful hunting party returns to the village and divides up the proceeds of the hunt. The proceeds are used to feed, clothe and shelter the village. Essentially, the hunt supplies the village with 100 percent of its material needs. Of course, villager disputes arise requiring arbitration. Marriages need to be officially sanctified and there are spiritual and medical needs as well. Someone must also perform the task of creating social order.

This role cannot go to anyone in the hunting party because the members of the hunting party are away for days at a time performing their hunting tasks. The village needs a government, so a chief is appointed. Since the chief cannot hunt, the chief is a financial burden to the village. The hunters in the hunting party not only have to procure enough deer for themselves and their families, they must also procure enough deer for the chief and her family. The chief generates zero deer because the chief does not hunt.

For the chief to exist, the hunting party must produce above and beyond the internal needs of the hunting party to support someone who does not contribute any food, clothing, shelter, or manufactured goods for the village. This production of deer, which is above and beyond the hunting party's internal needs, is called a profit. Without a profit (a procurement in excess of the needs of the hunting party) there could not be any chief.

The village might also need a medicine man to administer to the spiritual and health needs of the villagers. Again, this non-hunting occupation is a financial burden to the hunting party because the medicine man does not hunt. This places an additional profit burden on the hunting party. Now the hunting party must procure enough deer to feed themselves and their families, the chief and her family, and the medicine man and his family. Occasionally a hunter is injured on the hunt to the point where the hunter is disabled and can no longer produce. If the village agrees to support the disabled hunter then it places an additional financial burden on the hunting party as the disabled can no longer procure deer. The hunters must make more profit to support the disabled. Even if the decision to support the disabled hunter is made by the chief or medicine man, the disabled hunter still is a burden to the hunting party. If the disabled hunter is hired as a helper for the chief it still does not affect the additional profit burden placed upon the hunting party.

Should any of the villagers dislike the hunting party? Of course not! The hunting party provides the village with 100 percent of the village's food, clothing and manufactured goods—essentially everything. If the hunting party fails to complete its task then the villagers will all die. The reason there is a hunting party, as opposed to individual hunters, is because the task at hand can only be successfully and efficiently achieved by an organization. The hunting party exists because it is impossible to hunt the fast, elusive deer individually with a spear. Only by organizing into a group can the necessary tasks required to support the village succeed. The more the hunting party succeeds, the wealthier the village becomes. There is no other way for the village to become wealthy. The only thing a chief can do is ration the meat and by-products, but the chief cannot produce more meat per person. Only the hunting party has the capability to increase the meat and by-product per person. Only the hunting party can give the people better food, better clothing, and better shelter.

Should a political environment exist that allows too many chiefs or too much government then there will be too much burden on the hunting party and everyone in the village will suffer (except for the chief of course). The problem is compounded by a corrupt chief. Corruption of the chief occurs when the chief takes the proceeds of the hunting party and either retains the proceeds for personal gain or doles out the proceeds to maintain political power. Corruption or an anti-hunting party sentiment would certainly destroy or damage the overall prosperity of the village. No army conquered Rome, no army conquered the Soviet Union, they just collapsed upon the corrupt chiefs. Any action, sentiment, behavior or belief which does not support the hunting party 100 percent is counter-productive to the well being of the villagers.

It is impossible for the hunting party to be greedy. The concept of a greedy hunting party makes absolutely no sense because as the hunting party's profit increases it allows more prosperity. The chief does not provide medical services. It is the profit generated by the hunting party which allows the medicine man to exist. No profit equals no medicine man equals no health care. Third world kings never fly to Russia for medical treatment. They do not fly to England or Canada either. They fly to the United States because the United States generates the most profit, which affords the best medicine. The more profits generated by the hunting party, the better life is. Each villager should do everything possible to see to it the hunting party is in good order because their life depends upon it. The chief does not have any resources other than what the hunting party generates. The chief can provide temporary support, but eventually all wealth is derived from the hunting party.

The hunting party cannot go out of business. There are an infinite amount of deer in an infinite amount of forest on Planet Forest, therefore there is simply no reason not to hunt. Individual hunters will fail, but the village will not fail.

Not all hunting parties are nice. Not all hunters are nice, not all of the jobs in the hunting party are nice. Nice or not, the village will die without the proceeds of the hunting party. The hunters who are responsible to gut the freshly killed deer may not like their job. They may feel underpaid and under appreciated. They may form a union, the Deer Gutters Union. The union is not saying the hunting party is bad. The union knows without the hunting party there would be no union, there would be no village. The purpose of the union is simply to bargain with the leader of the hunting party for a greater share of the hunt. No rational villager is against the hunting party because every villager knows where their next meal is coming from.

The Modern Corporation

The modern corporation is identical to the hunting party of the village or the farming operation on Planet Corn. The corporation is formed because the business task at hand requires an organization to meet the challenges of the task; challenges which far exceed the capacity of the individual.

The task of mass producing an automobile requires an extremely large organization. Could an individual dig up 100 million tons of iron ore, ship it a thousand miles, unload it, melt it, pound it into shape, assemble the shape into cars, design an engine, insert plastic, acquire the skill to develop the onboard computer, etc. . . . ? The task of building automobiles requires hundreds of thousands of workers. The task requires a large organization, not a small group. Corporations are simply the hunting party performing a task which only a larger group can do. Big corporations are big because the task at hand requires the organization to be big enough to successfully meet the challenge of the task.

If it requires fifty hunters to surround a deer on Planet Forest in order to optimize the procurement of that deer, then the hunting party should have fifty hunters. A hunting party of fifty hunters best serves the village. If someone invents a bow and arrow which is technologically superior to the spear, then maybe thirty-five hunters can accomplish the same rate of efficiency as fifty spear-bearing hunters.

The hunting party would then lay off fifteen hunters who would need to do something other than hunting—perhaps bow and arrow manufacturing. The hunting party is not mean or cruel for laying off fifteen hunters. The hunting party is mathematically indifferent. For the village to survive, the hunting party must be efficient regardless of individual circumstances. The hunting party is an organization. An organization is not a person. An organization is an answer to a problem at hand. The problem at hand is solved by an organization of whatever size it takes to solve the problem. The size of the organization is constantly changing because the technology used to solve the problem is constantly changing.

There were once tens of thousands of coal miners. Now there are fewer miners, due to the invention of coal digging machines. In 1776, 95 percent of the United States population were farmers. In 1976, 5 percent of the population were farmers. What happened to all the farmers? The tractor happened. The modern day farmer just got laid off from the auto factory due to the invention of the robot and is now learning how to work with computers.

Corporations are big because the task at hand requires big. Some corporations are small because their size is a snapshot of their current position during their growth on the way to becoming big. Some corporations are small because the task at hand requires small. Some corporations are invented out of business. There are few wagon-wheel makers left. Some corporations fail because the manager whose job it is to operate the organization makes errors.

Not all corporations are well behaved. Not all hunting parties are well behaved either. Some jobs in corporations are no fun. Some jobs in hunting parties are no fun. Some individuals who work for corporations are of low moral character and behave poorly toward their colleagues. The same goes for the hunting party. Some jobs in corporations have higher compensation then others. It depends upon the skills of the particular individuals, and the value of skills change over time. There is currently little value in someone who can hit a running deer with a stone head spear seven out of ten times. Such a skill during the time of hunting parties would have been highly prized. The entrepreneurial talent so highly prized in some businesses is frowned upon in other businesses.

The value of skills changes from corporation to corporation. If the individual does not like her job at corporation A , then she can quit and go to corporation B. The corporation is not responsible for individual happiness. The individual is responsible for self-actualization.

The corporation is simply an organization of people joined for the purpose of completing a task, which can only be performed by a group. The purpose of the corporation is to do whatever the task is and do it as efficiently as possible in order to benefit the members of the corporation and to create a surplus of wealth which exceeds the immediate needs of its members. The surplus is essential to support those who do not contribute to the immediate needs of society. The hunting party must procure enough deer to feed, clothe, and shelter the chief who does not hunt, the medicine man, the injured hunter who cannot hunt, the teacher who teaches the young where neither the young or the teacher hunt, the old who can no longer hunt, and anyone who is not actively engaged in hunting.

The surplus, or profit, of the corporation is essential, just as the hunting party's surplus is essential. The function of the corporation is to generate as much profit as possible to support all of society. There cannot be enough profit—the more profit the better life is. The modern corporation must generate enough profit to support the teachers, members of the clergy, politicians, doctors, the old, the sick the stay at home parent, the children, or anyone who is not actively involved in production. It is only the profit of corporations which enable teachers, inventors, doctors, nurses, members of the clergy, politicians, unemployed parents, babies, and the disabled to exist.

The Ice Age villager's 401(k) plan is a piece of ice pushed out into warm water with the retiree on board. It is a one-way ticket to the happy hunting ground. These preindustrial villagers are not cruel, uncaring people; they simply cannot produce enough excess walrus (profit) to care for every non-hunter. No one in the modern world ices their retirees because there is a steel mill in central Pennsylvania making a profit, or a mining company in West Virginia making a profit which covers the cost of a non producer from Anywhere, USA. Without corporate profit there would be no retirement, education, invention, or hospitals. There would be no access to medical care, no religion; there would be nothing but work. Without profit there would be nothing but work and the day you stopped working would be the day you die. Without corporate profit your uneducated child would die a premature death because there would be no teacher to teach him and there would be no doctor to administer care.

It is nonsensical to say a corporation is greedy or makes too much profit as it is the profit which provides every citizen with 100 percent of everything a citizen has. The profit of corporations is the only source of wealth. There is no other source. There is no other wealth created other then what is created by corporations via the profit generated from production. Total production less what is needed to operate the corporation is profit. Without profit there would be no invention. Following human invention through history is the same as following the most profitable societies. Unprofitable societies invent nothing and profitable societies invent almost everything. The prime meridian is an invisible line running through Greenwich, England. It is used to navigate earth as well as establish exact time. The line was established in England because at the time England was the richest country in the world. The English thought God must be an Englishman because the English were inventing so much at that time. When the empire ended so did the invention. God did not leave, the corporate profits did.

The corporation, like the hunting party, is the procurer of 100 percent of every material good a citizen has. Corporate profits also enable nonmaterial concepts to exist such as art, philosophy, and religion. Virtually all production is created by corporations and production is wealth. Production is accounted for in units of currency. Currency is not production. Currency is not wealth. Wealth is production. Currency is only a simple tool to measure real production. The use of currency in a society is called measurementism.

The investor must understand the difference between money and wealth. To accumulate wealth is to accumulate ownership in production or ownership in a corporation. If you live on Planet Corn, wealth is measured by how much corn producing land you own. In the hunting village wealth is measured by how much of the hunt you own, and on earth wealth is measured by how much corporate ownership you have, and to own corporations you must purchase stock. The 500 largest corporations control 80 percent of the wealth in the United States. The remaining 14,500 smaller corporations control approximately 18 percent, leaving only 2 percent outside corporate control. Therefore, 98 percent of the nation's wealth is determined by corporate ownership, and to own all or part of a corporation the investor must own stock.

Whatever reduces corporate profits reduces the standard of living of all citizens.

The Role of Government

The role of government in modern society is identical to the chief in the hunting village. The government and everyone one in it is a burden to production because government produces nothing. The source of wealth or the source of production is corporations. Corporations must give some of their proceeds to the government. Actually, the government requires part of corporate proceeds be given to the government, which is the only way the government obtains money. The hunting party must produce enough deer to enable the members of the hunting party to live and the hunting party must also produce in excess of its needs to support the non-hunters such as the chief. Corporations must produce enough to support the activities of the corporation and produce in excess of their internal needs to pay the required governmental tax. Therefore 100 percent of tax revenue to the government is from corporate profits. There is no other source of tax revenue other than from corporate profits.

Everyone in society lives off of corporate profits. The government receives 100 percent of its revenue from corporate tax (taxing the corporation directly) and income tax, which is taxing the individual citizen who earns his income from corporate profits. If the chief in the hunting village takes too many hunters out of production, the entire village will suffer. The government must be careful to only bleed the corporation, but not kill it. If the blood-sucking leech sucks too much blood then both the leech and host animal die. The government must be careful not to absorb too much production to the point where it damages the welfare of the citizens. An example of bleeding corporations too much is exhibited in socialist countries. Socialist countries are significantly less well off because their production has been lowered by too much government tax.

The government must keep order, resolve disputes, and print money. The real cost of government is understood by the amount of corporate production which must be reduced to accommodate governmental needs. The reduction of corporate production has a direct effect in making all citizens poorer because 100 percent of everything a citizen has is from corporate profits.

Corrupt government is a constant and real threat to the welfare of the people. Judea, Rome, the Ottoman Empire, the USSR, and the British Empire all fell because of weak governments, not external challenges. Government reduces wealth. Some government is necessary to establish order, but every dollar spent on government is one less dollar of production, assuming all the laws created either increase production or are neutral toward production. Most laws do not help production.

Government is a necessary wealth-reducing evil.

One of the most common misinformation tricks of the evil side of government is use of the term "federal money." The term implies that "federal money" originated from the government and the government solved problem xyz by applying federal money to the problem. The government makes zero money, creates zero money, and has no power to earn money. The government simply takes money from the profits of corporations. The source of all money is from the production of corporations. Any and all problems solved by money are solved by corporate profits. Those who benefit from a solution that was solved by applying money to it should thank the source of all money: corporations.

One Choice

There is only one investment choice. It appears there are hundreds of investment choices and different ways to invest but really there is only one. Hundreds of businesses offer an unimaginable list of investment choices referred to by a hundred different names. But regardless of the terminology, there is still only one investment choice. Finance is simple in concept, but its simplicity is clouded by the abundance of terms. The only investment choice is to invest in the source of wealth. If an investor lives on Planet Corn then the only source of wealth is corn production. If the investor is a villager on Planet Forest then the only source of wealth is the proceeds of the hunting party. On Earth the only source of wealth is corporate profits. All investment choices are a form of corporate profits. The investment return is a result of both the performance of the corporation in generating a rate of profit and the contract or agreement, which explains what type of corporate profit or what percentage of the corporate profit the investor will receive. All rates of return on all investments are 100 percent paid for by corporate profits.

All wealth is derived from one source: corporate profits. Production which generates wealth in excess of the internal needs of the producing corporation is corporate profits. All investment returns are some type of corporate profit. Some investments only receive a portion of corporate profits and some investments receive 100 percent of corporate profits. See the following list of investments where some only receive a small percentage of profits and others receive 100 percent of corporate profits.

Investments which receive a small percentage of corporate profits:

(a) Bank savings account
(b) Bank certificates of deposit
(c) Any bank account which pays interest
(d) Money market
(e) Federal government bonds
(f) State and municipal government bonds

(g) Corporate bonds
(h) All insurance products which pay a return
 (i) All mutual funds which pay some type of interest
 (j) Annuities
(k) Social Security

Investments which receive 100 percent of corporate profits:

(a) Stocks
(b) Stock mutual funds

The investor decides what percentage of corporate profit she will receive by the choice of investments. Some investments pay the investor very little and some investments pay substantially. The investments which pay small returns do so because the particular investment is only entitled to receive a portion of corporate profits. The investments with a substantial return pay handsomely because they receive 100 percent of corporate profits.

An investor who at age thirty-six made a one-time deposit of $10,000 would have the money grow in 30 years to the following amounts:

$10,000 INVESTED IN:	→	TOTAL ASSETS 30 YRS LATER
Social Security	→	$13,300
Money Market Fund	→	$23,000
Microsoft Bond	→	$41,000
Microsoft Stock	→	$7,000,000

All four investments had 100 percent of their gains paid for by corporate profits. Only one of the investments received 100 percent of corporate profits and the other three only received a small portion of corporate profits. The investment with $7 million in gains received 100 percent of corporate profits while the other three scenarios only received a small percentage.

Stocks, Bonds, and Money

There is only one source of wealth in the United States. The only source of wealth is the production from corporations and the resulting corporate profits. An investor can either receive 100 percent of corporate profits or receive some percentage of corporate profits. An investor who purchases ownership in a corporation is paid back by receiving 100 percent of corporate profits based upon his or her percentage of ownership. Lending money to a corporation is a very different arrangement. The lender lends money to a corporation and is paid back by receiving only a small percentage of corporate profits.

The lender to corporations is a creditor. When an investor lends money to a corporation, such as Ford Motor, the corporation (Ford) goes into debt by the amount lent. If the investor lends Ford $1000 then Ford is indebted for $1000 and must pay the lender/investor back. The terms of the promise to pay the lender back with interest are written on a piece of paper called a corporate bond. When an investor lends money to a corporation the investor receives a bond in exchange for her money.

A bond investor therefore buys bonds or corporate IOUs. Buying a bond is simply lending money to a corporation with the expectation the corporation will make enough profit to take care of the internal needs of the corporation, to pay taxes (which is typically more than one half of the profits), to spend on research to maintain or gain its competitive advantage, and, finally, to grow and pay off its lenders (bond investors). Without corporate profits the bond investor receives nothing.

The problem with lending money to corporations is the corporations can only pay the lender back from a small percentage of corporate profits. It is impossible to pay the lender (bond buyer/investor) 100 percent of profits because much of the profit is prescheduled to meet other obligations. If it takes 100 percent of corporate profits to meet the debt obligation of the outstanding bonds, then the corporation will go out of business. The business will fail because bond debt payment is just one of many responsibilities the corporation must meet with corporate profits.

The bond buyer is told in advance exactly what interest rate will be paid and when the bond will mature. The buyer of the bond will receive the bond with 5 percent written on it, for example, and with the length of time stipulated for the payback. For example, the bond buyer knows he will receive a fixed rate of interest on the loan of 5 percent over some period of time. If the growth rate of the company is 20 percent, the bond investor does not receive any amount extra. The bond investor is locked into the fixed interest rate which must be less then the growth rate of the corporation. Regardless of how fast the corporation grows, the bond buyer does not gain from the growth other than from receiving the fixed interest.

The long-term rate of return of bonds is approximately half the long-term rate of return of ownership as expressed in stocks. If the long-term growth rate of U.S. corporations is 11 percent, then bonds must be half of 11 percent or 5.5 percent. Bonds must always pay the investor half the rate of ownership, on average. Bonds never participate in the growth rate of a corporation because the return on bonds is fixed. This is why an investor in Microsoft bonds who invested $10,000 in 1973 and held the bonds until 2002 would have $41,000 while the stock investor who invested the same $10,000 would have $7 million by 2002. Even if the corporation has a very fast growth rate, the bond investor only receives his or her fixed rate of return and does not participate in any of the growth.

Money Market Accounts

Money market accounts are referred to by many different terms, such as savings account, cash account, bank account, money market fund, etc. The average investor confuses a money market account with currency. Currency, or cash, is not an investment; the green stuff in a wallet is currency, which is used for the purpose of exchange. A money market fund is not currency. Currency is used to purchase short-term corporate bonds and the bonds pay the interest rate received by the money market fund. An investor who deposits $1,000 of currency into a money market account actually exchanges the currency for very short-term corporate bonds or corporate debt. The currency is used to purchase thirty- to ninety-day IOUs from hundreds of different corporations. Whatever interest is paid to the depositor is paid by corporate profits. These thirty- to ninety-day corporate IOUs are the method by which corporations satisfy their short-term financial needs. Deposits of currency are not simply dropped into a vault for safekeeping. Currency is only used for purposes of exchange. Therefore it earns no interest and is constantly depreciating in value due to inflation. If a depositor deposited $500 in currency into a box in 1931 for the purpose of buying a new Cadillac in 1980 the depositor would discover the $500, which at one time could buy a Cadillac, can now only cover the price of tires. The $500 depreciated due to inflation and did not earn any interest because currency is only used for exchange purposes. Currency is not entitled to receive any corporate profits.

Money market funds are not currency stored in a vault. Deposited currency into a money market fund is exchanged for short-term corporate bonds. Therefore a money market fund is a bond fund which has very little fluctuation because the bonds mature in thirty to ninety days. As the time between the date issued and the date the investor is paid the principal increases so does the interest rate. Ninety-day bonds pay much less interest then five-year bonds. However, both money market funds and bond funds are still corporate IOUs and 100 percent of the rate of return to the investor is paid by corporate profits.

Certificates of Deposit

Bank CDs are also corporate bonds. When an investor deposits currency into a bank for the purpose of buying a CD, the investor is actually buying a bond fund. The bank buys corporate bonds with the currency and the corporations pay the bank via corporate profits. The corporate bonds pay the bank interest, the bank keeps a little for itself and pays the depositor the difference. The fact remains that 100 percent of the rate of return of the CD is paid for by corporate profits. No matter what an investment product is called, it is always paid for by corporate profits.

Stocks

An ownership certificate in a corporation is called a share of stock. If an investor owns 50 percent of the outstanding shares of stock then the investor owns 50 percent of the corporation. Whatever percent of the outstanding stock the investor owns is the percentage of ownership. Each share of stock participates equally in the profits plus the growth rate of the corporation. If an investor buys a share of stock in a corporation and the corporation gains in value then each share gains equally. If the corporation doubles in value then each individual share of stock will double. If an investor buys one share for one dollar and the stock doubles, then the investor's stock is worth two dollars. The investment of a wealthier investor buying $50 million worth of the same stock which doubles will therefore increase to $100 million. All investors are paid in equal percentage gains.

The stock owner is literally and legally the owner of the corporation she purchased stock in. As owner, the stockholder receives 100 percent of all gains and losses. The gains are without limit and the losses are limited to the purchase price of the stock.

If an investor deposited $1000 in currency into a lock box in 1925, by 2001 it would be worth $105, due to inflation.[1] One thousand dollars in 1925 would only be worth $105 seventy-six years into the future. The 1925 bill would have $1000 written on it but it could only buy $105 worth of goods. The same $1000 in currency exchanged for a thirty- to ninety-day corporate IOU (money market) would have grown to $16,000 over 76 years, a five- to ten-year bond would have grown to $40,000 and the same amount invested in stocks would grow somewhere between $2 to $7 million, depending upon which size corporation the money was invested in.[2]

Stocks can earn more than any other investment because, as owner, the stockholder is entitled to 100 percent of corporate gains. The bondholder (holder of corporate IOUs) only receives a fraction of corporate gains. The long-term investor simply needs to choose which amount of money he would prefer to have: a lot or a little. Stocks can receive a lot of corporate profits and bonds receive a little.

---

[1]U.S. Department of Labor.
[2]Ibbotson and Associates. *SBBI 2003 Yearbook Market Results for 1926–2003: Stocks, Bonds, Bills and Inflation.* Chicago: Ibbotson Associates.

The Gross Domestic Product and Stocks

Accroding to the U.S. Department of Commerce, the Gross Domestic Product (GDP) is the value of goods and services produced by labor and property in the United States, regardless of nationality (foreign owned businesses in the United States are included in the GDP measure). "Gross" means all, "domestic" means the United States, and "product" means production. Gross Domestic Product is therefore the total value of U.S. production.

From 1929 to 2002, the growth rate of the Gross Domestic Product was approximately 9.53 percent. Over the same period of time, the annualized growth rate of the S&P 500 was 9.73 percent. The two rates of return are so similar, they are virtually indistinguishable. The indistinguishability is due to how the inflation rate is estimated, because the Gross Domestic Product is calculated by using an estimate of inflation, and the stock market establishes the rate of inflation via free market valuation. In addition, the government has changed the methodology of how the Gross Domestic Product is calculated. The two measures, Gross Domestic Product being a calculation by the U.S. Department of Commerce and the stock market as defined as the S&P 500 is measured by the free market, are not exact because they are calculated differently, but both measure the same thing—corporate profits.

The rate of return of the Gross Domestic Product and the stock market, which is commonly referred to as the S&P 500, are the same because the GDP and S&P 500 are literally the same. Both the GDP and S&P 500 are simply measures of total corporate profits. The Department of Commerce measures total corporate profits and provides the measure to the public as the national rate of growth of the economy.

The government estimates the value of the economy every three months whereas the stock market places a real dollar price valuation on corporate profits every second during market hours: 9:30 AM to 4:00 PM Monday through Friday.

The free market does the exact same thing by measuring corporate profits via the valuation of stock prices. The free market valuation is the stock market and the government measurement is an estimate. The estimate and free market valuation should be extremely similar over time, but will diverge over shorter periods of time.

The following graph shows the growth rate of the GDP to be very steady over time.

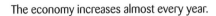

The economy increases almost every year.

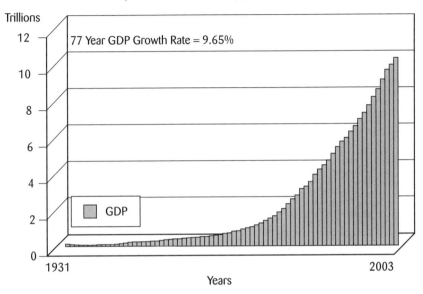

The Growth Rate of the GDP 1931 to 2003

Source: U.S. Department of Commerce.

During the bear market of 2000–2002, the large cap stock market declined approximately 10 percent in 2000, 11 percent in 2001 and 24 percent in 2002. The declining market ignored the rising GDP over the same time period. The GDP gained approximately 6.7 percent over the three-year bear market in which the S&P 500 declined over 40 percent. Corporate profits gained 6.7 percent but stock prices fell 40 percent. The cause of the short term disconnect is simply because the natural fluctuation of the free market occasionally over pays and under pays for stocks while actual corporate profits, as measured by the GDP, steadily move forward.

Compare the following three graphs. The ups and downs of the first graph depict the large cap stock market changing year to year. The second graph illustrates how little the Gross Domestic Product changes; it is almost always positive. The third graph shows how the stock market follows the growth of the Gross Domestic Product. Both the stock market and the GDP measure the same thing: corporate profits. Therefore, both have the same long term rates of growth. The stock market will have much greater short-term volatility because it is subject to speculative bidding up and selling down due to investor sentiments. The volatility rate (standard deviation) of the Gross Domestic Product is 5.2 percent and the standard deviation of the large cap stock market is approximately 20 percent.

The long-term investor in corporate profits can see that economic growth is actually very steady; much steadier than the stock market would indicate on a short-term basis. Investors have only one way to purchase into the 10 percent growth rate of the economy and that is to buy stock. This is why investment professionals advise investors not to worry when stock prices fall. Eventually, stock prices mirror the GDP.

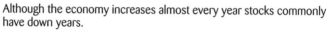

Although the economy increases almost every year stocks commonly have down years.

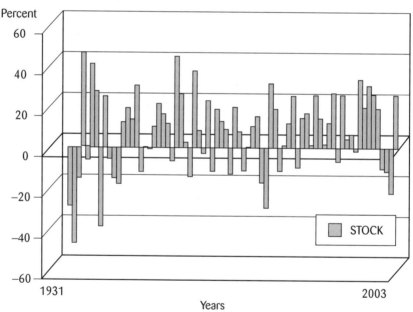

The Gains and Losses of the Gross Domestic Product Plus Inflation Year to Year

Source: Standard & Poors. Subsidiary of McGraw-Hill. South Brunswick, N.J.: Dow Jones & Company.

The economy increases almost every year as measured by the Gross Domestic Product.

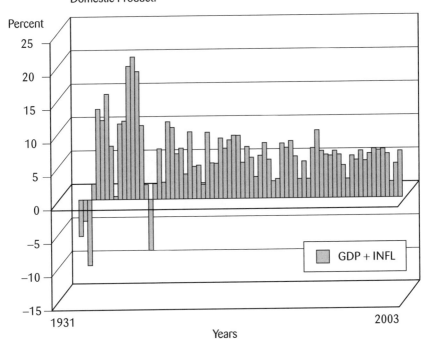

The Gains and Losses of the Gross Domestic Product Plus Inflation Year to Year

Source: U.S. Department of Commerce.

The economy increases year to year as measured by the Gross Domestic Product and the stock market follows the same growth pattern because the value of stocks and the value of the Gross Domestic Product are the same thing. They both measure corporate profits.

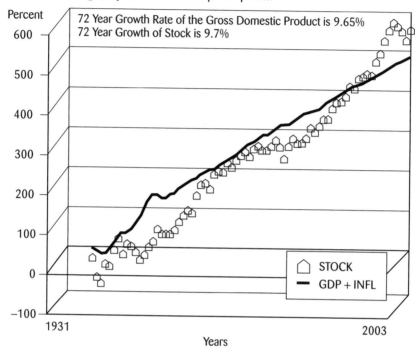

Comparison of the Long-Term Growth of the Gross Domestic Product and the Stock Market

Source: U.S. Department of Commerce; Standard & Poors. Subsidiary of McGraw-Hill. South Brunswick, N.J.: Dow Jones & Company.

What Are the Risks of Stocks, Bonds, Money Markets, and Currency?

R isk is a broad concept which is impossible to either describe or explain in a single word. The commonly understood meaning equates risk to a permanent loss. The investor has $50 in his pocket and bets it all on horse number 7 at the local racetrack and horse number 7 loses. The $50 is now an unrecoverable zero. The investor placed the $50 at risk and lost it. "Risk" is perceived as the same as "loss" in the minds of many investors. There is a perception of danger when putting money into either the stock or bond markets. This perception is of no use to a participant in a 401(k) who is forty-years-old and has but one investment choice: corporate profits.

In the typical profit sharing/401(k) plan, investors have only one choice in which to invest and that choice is corporate profits. Since all wealth is created from corporate profits, then all investment returns are paid by corporate profits. What is the risk of all corporate profits going to zero? Understanding risk is understanding how corporate profits are paid out to lenders and owners of corporate assets. There is not any possibility that all corporations will all go out of business at the same time.

What is the risk of the hunting party never catching another deer on Planet Forest? Planet Forest offers an unlimited supply of deer in millions of square miles of forest. What are the chances of the hunting party experiencing a 100 percent failure rate in a forest full of deer? The deer population is limitless just as human creativity is limitless in its capacity to solve problems. There is zero chance all the corn farmers on Planet Corn will just decide to sit down in their fertile fields, not plant any corn, and universally agree to starve to death. There is zero chance all the hunters with loved ones they are responsible to feed, clothe, and shelter would collectively decide not to hunt and just sit down and passively starve themselves and their families. Their wives would not tolerate it.

There is also zero chance all corporations will simultaneously fail and all corporate profits will go to zero. Since there is only one investment choice, corporate profits, and corporate profits never fail, then corporate profits have no risk. Corporate profits in aggregate cannot fail but individual corporations can. There is risk in investing and there is also zero risk in investing. Avoiding risk and obtaining wealth are a result of understanding how corporate profits function in modern society over time. An investor who purchased $1000 worth of stock in a single corporation is at risk for a 100 percent loss, because individual companies commonly fail.

If 100 percent of an investor's assets are in a failed corporate stock, then the assets are lost. If 100 percent of an investor's assets are in a failed corporate bond then the assets are lost. Avoiding risk is accomplished by spreading the assets over several hundred corporations, as it is impossible for the entire universe of corporations to fail. Diversifying creates zero chance of a total loss.

Individual corporations can fail. A corporate failure has virtually no aggregate impact on society. A business failure has no impact on the nation in total because there are hundreds of other businesses doing the exact same function. A business fails because it cannot, for whatever reason, generate enough profit to pay its workers, pay for plant and equipment, research, pay the owners, and pay the government 50 percent of its total income.

A business does not fail because everything is fine. A business fails because everything is not ok. The failure does not have any impact on society because there are ten other businesses doing the exact same function which will replace the work of the failed business and, typically, eagerly and more efficiently do it better. Society loses nothing, although the individuals who were members of the failed business must find another business and, other than the irritation of the people who worked for the failed company, society and diversified investors suffer no ill effect. Not only does a business failure not hurt society, 99 percent of the time it improves society's standards as a whole.

If there were ten wagon wheel makers in 1901 producing a million wheels per year and one of the makers was a poor business person whose business failed, then the other nine would rapidly make up the production and the wagon wheel buyers would still have the same production rate of one million wheels at essentially the same price or even less. The price could decline because the less efficient maker was gone and the remaining makers were more efficient. More wagon wheel failures could occur because several makers might invent a significantly superior production process that puts several more companies out of business. The consumer would gain because of the lower price.

Henry Ford entered the competition and invented the mass produced automobile. As a consequence, he put all the wagon wheel makers, along with the black smiths, saddle makers, rawhide salesmen, horse breeders, and most veterinarians out of business. Ford's inventiveness put 30 percent of the U.S. economy out of business while simultaneously replacing it with a more profitable industry, making the nation more wealthy.

Business failures are typical, normal, and part of society's growth process. There should not be any fear of business failures for the long-term diversified investor. As long as the investor learns to eliminate the risk of bankruptcy by not overinvesting in any single corporation, then the risk of individual business failure can be completely eliminated. If the investor is invested in a hundred different large corporations then a few bankruptcies are irrelevant and expected. The long-term growth of an economy is not only unaffected by bankruptcy, but progress would be impossible without the failure of weak, inefficient, and obsolete businesses.

The return from all investments is 100 percent paid for from corporate profits. The investor chooses the manner in which the corporate profits are paid out. There are only two ways for the investor to receive corporate profits. One, the investor can receive 100 percent of the profits from a corporation, or two, the investor can receive some percentage or an amount less then 100 percent of corporate profits.

Choice one, receiving 100 percent of corporate profits, is achieved by becoming a legal owner of the corporation. As owner, the investor is entitled to all of the gains and losses of the business. Ownership of large corporations is sold in percentages and the investor can purchase any percentage of ownership desired up to 100 percent, resources permitting. Most investors cannot buy all of General Motors so they settle for a small percentage. Corporate ownership is sold in shares of stock: if the investor buys 1 percent of the shares of stock then the investor owns 1 percent of the corporation. It does not make any difference whether the investor buys 1 percent or one millionth of 1 percent; all shares of stock in a given business pay investors an equal rate of return per share. Just because some own more stock then others does not entitle them to a higher payout. All returns are equal. If Ford Motor Company pays its stockholders (owners) a 5 percent dividend, then each share receives 5 percent. If the share price either advances or declines all of the shareholders again share equally.

The maximum possible rate of return of any investment is equal to the growth rate of corporate profits in a single corporation. The worst case scenario is when all assets are invested in a single corporation and the corporation fails. The worst case scenario for an investor spread over the top 500 U.S. corporations is zero long-term risk. The top 500 U.S. corporations essentially are the economy and the investor will forever have a positive growth rate as long as the country exists. The long-term annualized rate of return of stocks is approximately 10 to 11 percent. Therefore, the typical diversified investor should earn something similar to 10 to 11 percent over the long run.

The only other form of corporate profits an investor can invest in are bonds. Lending money to a corporation obligates the corporation to do two things. One, pay the investor back the money which was lent at some future date, and two, also pay some rate of interest. Buying a bond is simply lending money to a corporation. To buy a one thousand dollar-General Electric bond is to lend $1000 to GE. GE promises to pay back the $1000 plus an amount of interest. On average, the lending rate of return (interest paid) must be approximately half the average long-term corporate profit rate of growth. If the average long-term bond return is 5.5 percent then the average corporate profit should be twice 5.5 percent or 11 percent. Bond investors are paid only a percentage of corporate profits, but not all corporate profits. Interest due bond investors is only one of the many obligations a corporation has. If a corporation is growing at 20 percent per year then the owner receives 20 percent and the bond investor receives her interest rate, for example 5 percent. If the corporate profits are 100 percent, the owner receives 100 percent and the bond investor receives 5 percent. The bond investor receives a fixed amount of interest and does not participate in the growth of the business.

The investor is paid by corporate profits no matter what the investment choice: stocks, bonds, and money markets are all paid by corporate profits. Government bonds are also paid for by corporate profits. The government taxes the corporation and uses the tax proceeds to pay back the investor. The promise of the government to pay the investor back is only as good as the income stream of corporate profits. If there were not any corporate profits then there would not be any government. The government meets all of its financial obligations with corporate profits. Social Security, food stamps, unemployment, Medicare, all forms of welfare, military expenditures, limos for politicians, etc. are all paid for by corporate profits. Corporate profits pay for everything.

Some dishonest politicians and their supporters in the public perpetuate the idea the origin of money is the government. They use trick words such as, "What guarantee does the stock market provide?" or "Isn't Social Security better if it is guaranteed by the government?" The reality is the government does not have the power to guarantee anything. The government and everyone else in society receives 100 percent of all wealth from corporate profits. The only guarantee for the future is from corporate profit.

Currency is what most people refer to as money. Currency is used as a common standardized measure of corporate profits to trade x for y. The currency itself has no real value other than what we agree to give it. The amount of currency in circulation must be roughly equal to the corporate profits generated or the value of currency becomes either too high or too low. As the government typically prints more currency then there is production to justify, the currency constantly decreases in value.

The ongoing problem with currency is it constantly shrinks in value, meaning it takes more currency to buy a given good or service from year to year. If an investor locked up $1000 in a lock box for thirty years, the $1000 would shrink in value at the rate of inflation. This means $1000 locked up in the present with the expectation it could buy a new car will be insufficient in the future when the car costs $5000. The value of the currency shrunk to $200 of real value from its original value of $1000. To put it another way, it will take five times as much currency thirty years into the future to buy a similar good or service in the present.[3] Currency is extremely risky and is constantly losing value because the government overprints it.

As all investments are a form of corporate profits and there is no investment which is not 100 percent paid for by corporate profits, the source of wealth is therefore corporate profit. Corporate profits pay 100 percent of Social Security, all government entitlements, every hat, shoe, house, ear of corn, everything. Corporate profits pay for every profession which does not create corporate profits: artists, teachers, members of the clergy, soldiers, politicians, entertainers, fiction writers, retirees, retirement workers—everything and everybody.

The future has but a single guarantee. The money in the future will be derived 100 percent from corporate profits and nowhere else. A Social Security check twenty years from now will be 100 percent paid for by corporate profits.

Investments in corporate profits, if spread over several 100 large businesses, do not have any risk. America's wealth is equal to its corporate wealth. The only power America has is the power of the wealth which corporations create from corporate profits. Communism lost to measurementism because communism could not generate enough profit to compete with a measurementistic society. Stocks therefore do not have any risk because the largest 500 U.S. corporations are our wealth. Only if the United States was hit by a great meteor or fell under the corrupt spell of non-measurementism or socialism could corporate profits fail. The future is corporate profits: protect profits or die, or worse, live in squalor.

---

[3] U.S. Department of Commerce.

Short-term changes in the price of securities do cause short-term losses only if the security is sold during a down market. As time increases, short-term losses change into long-term gains; these temporary declines can only be understood in terms of time.

Properly diversified stocks will suffer short-term losses. However, in time the losses turn to gains. The growth of corporate profits will always go up, but not every day, not every week, month or year, and not even every few years, but certainly every ten years or so. The real risk to stocks is time. Stocks always go up, but not necessarily over short periods of time. The long-term investor therefore does not have any risk.

Time

All wealth, all money, all goods and services are derived from a single source: corporate profits. Open the factory door and money pours out. Actually, open the factory door and a lump of steel flows out, or an automobile flows out. The value of the good or service that flows out of the corporate activity is measured and a corresponding amount of currency is printed. Society then has x amount of currency to meet its daily needs. When a million dollars worth of goods and services is generated by corporate activity, then a million dollars worth of currency is printed and put into circulation.

As all money and all wealth flows exclusively from corporate profits, then the only possible investment rate of return an investor can obtain is the return of corporate profits. All rates of return paid to investors are 100 percent paid for by corporate profits. Corporate profits always flow, there are always corporate profits, and there is not any risk that all corporate profits will stop flowing all at the same time. The flow of corporate profits is consistent over long periods of time, but inconsistent over shorter periods of time. Consistency of return or risk on investments is then understood in terms of time. Inconsistency of the flow of corporate profits over time is the risk to investing. A dollar invested (properly diversified) will always be worth a dollar or more in the future, given so much time.

Corporate profits always increase over time, but the rate of growth varies as corporate profits or production increase. The amount of time involved during the length of the variation is the short-term risk of investing. There is not any long-term risk of positive corporate profits. There is equally no long-term risk to investor returns as profits equal returns; they are one and the same.

Understanding investment risk is therefore understanding time. All markets go up, but not every day, month, or year. The investor can choose how much time exposure to a down period is tolerable. Eventually, a particular category of corporate business goes up. However, various categories have differing lengths of time when returns are negative.

Expected future rates of return are related to time. A very low rate of return is likely to have almost no time when a negative return occurs. As the rate of return increases, so then does the length of time where negative returns can occur. As the investor pursues long-term financial objectives with x amount of an expected rate of return, the investor must also accept that the resulting rate of return x will experience a time of negative returns.[4] It is impossible to earn a positive rate of return where the source of the earnings are corporate profits and avoid some short-term negatives.[5] Every positive return has times when negative returns occur.

The following table illustrates the relationship between expected rate of return and the exposure to the amount of time which negative returns can occur.

Rate of Return	Years for a Dollar to Recover Back to a Dollar
1%	0 years
3%	less than one year
5%	4 years
7%	5–7 years
10%	10 years
12%	15 years
14%	Unpredictable

The following example provides a practical picture of the preceding information. If a forty-two-year-old person wanted $250,000 at age sixty-five and had $364 to invest per month, then earning a rate of return of 7 percent per year would accomplish the goal. The investor must accept the fact that the positive 7 percent rate of return can and most likely will experience somewhere around a five-year period of time of negative returns. The investment will not grow at exactly 7 percent every year. Some years the return might be 11 percent, some years it might be −2 percent. Over time, market XYZ is expected to earn 7 percent on average. There is not any long-term risk to the 7 percent expected return. However, even with a 7 percent average annualized

---

[4]Sharp, William F. 1964 "Capital Asset Prices: A Theory of Market Equilibrium Under Conditions of Risk." *Journal of Finance*, xix.
[5]U.S. Department of Commerce.

rate of growth, there will be some years of negative returns. The worst case scenario (in a market with a 7 percent expected rate of return) is to experience five to seven years of negative returns as it takes five to seven years to fully recover from any loss. The exposure to the amount of time where negative returns can transpire is the risk incurred to pursue a 7 percent long-term rate of return.[6]

An investor at age forty-two who is expecting to work another twenty-three years is being too conservative in pursuing a 7 percent rate of return. A down market of only five years cannot possibly damage a twenty-three-year target.

It would be more rational for a forty-two-year-old person with a twenty-three-year time horizon to pursue a higher rate of return because the investor has the time to bridge a down market of at least ten years, for example, and earn a much higher rate of return, as well as gain an additional $100,000. A ten-year threat of a low return cannot hurt a twenty-three-year target.

Investors should know how many years into the future assets can be invested and then make certain the time exposure to a potential down period is less than the target. Do not expose assets to a market that has a fifteen year recovery time two years before retirement.

Investors can choose any long-term expected rate of return between zero and 12 percent with reasonable accuracy.

Each rate of return, 1 through 12 percent, will have an expected amount of time when the rate of return will be negative. As the expected rate of returns increases, so does the amount of time where negative returns increase. The most essential variable in understanding investing is time. If the investor understood in advance a prospective mutual fund XYZ had a 40 percent standard deviation and could take twenty years to recover from a down cycle, then the investor might reject the fund upon learning of its twenty year cycle.[7]

During my many years as a pension consultant I observed far too many sixty-year-olds who were at risk for a ten to fifteen year down cycle while they were only a few years from retirement. They were completely unaware of the number of years it would take to recover should the market experience a downturn.

―――――――

[6]Standard and Poors; Thomson Financial; Ibbotson and Associates.
[7]U.S. Department of Commerce.

Risk, Volatility, Zigzag, and Standard Deviation

The modern industrial free society must have a positive long-term growth rate to exist. Any society that cannot move forward quickly disappears. Or, most likely the government overseeing the society will fail if the corporate profits generated are insufficient to maintain the government.

Over the centuries the failure rate of large relatively free societies is extremely low. Greece failed around 200 BC and Rome ended around AD 500. Other than the Greeks and Romans, no other large democracy has gone out of business. Fear of societal failure is, based on human history, irrational.

When the investor is making long-term financial plans, the fear, or perceived risk of the United States failing, must be eliminated as a variable in the decision-making process.

The long-term growth rate of society is positive, meaning it always goes up. The rate of growth is calculated by adding the population growth rate plus the productivity improvement rate and then subtracting the drag of government. This growth rate is approximately 10 to 11 percent and as long as the country exists the long-term growth will remain. The long-term investor can therefore expect corporate profits to grow on average 10 percent. Some corporate profits grow faster and some slower, making the average around 10 percent. A thirty-five-year-old person managing her assets in a 401(k) or profit sharing plan should pursue a rate of return similar to the growth rate of society, not more and certainly not less.

The maximum possible rate of return that an industrial society offers the long-term investor is in the 12 to 14 percent range. The range of rate of return choices begins with zero percent and ends around 12 percent. Each investor can choose his future expected rate of return: 1 percent, 2 percent, 5 percent, 7 percent, 10 percent, 12 percent, or higher.[8] The structure of

---

[8]"Historical Behavior of Asset Returns," by Campbell R. Harvey, J. Paul Sticht, Professor of International Business, Foqua School of Business, Duke University.

finance will offer society a range of differing long-term expected rate or return choices.

Each rate of return choice has statistical behavioral attributes associated with it. A rate of return has three behavioral characteristics: time, return, and standard deviation. The term *standard deviation* means average rate of change: *standard* means average and *deviation* means change. If a rate of return x has a standard deviation of 10 percent it means the expected growth rate is $+(x)$ and in any given year $+(x)$ can decline 10 percent or gain 10 percent. Since x is a positive number, the rate of return will always increase over time, but not every year. The average expected worst case is a loss of 10 percent in a given year and the average expected best case return is a gain of 10 percent where the rate of return is typically half or less than the standard deviation.[9]

If the standard deviation is 10 percent then the expected rate of return is typically half, or 5 percent. Any investor who pursues a long-term positive rate of return must face the fact of occasional negative return years. How many negative years? The exposure to negative years increases as the expected return increases. An investor with a 10 percent target rate of return will experience more down years then an investor with a 5 percent target.

Imagine viewing a graphical illustration of a sound wave. During complete silence the sound wave is a straight line. As the noise level increases, the zigzag increases. Imagine viewing a seismograph when the earth is not moving. Then as an earthquake becomes larger, the zigzag on the seismograph becomes larger. Big noise: big zigzag. Big earthquake: big zigzag.

A zero rate of return is the same as no sound or a still earth. No zigzag is the same as nothing. Big rate of return: big zigzag.[10]

A 10 percent target rate of return will have a higher standard deviation than a 5 percent target rate of return. An investor who attempts to earn 10 percent per year will face the reality of a 20 percent standard deviation. This means in any given year the assets may decline 20 percent or grow 20 percent. Standard deviation is expressed as an annualized number and is an average risk behavioral characteristic. Standard deviation is an estimation which is incorrect approximately five years per century. Therefore, a 10 percent target rate of return with a 20 percent standard deviation is expected to have as a normal occurrence occasional 20 percent losses.

---

[9]Thomson Financial, Rockville, MD.
[10]"Indicator Analysis." www.stockcharts.com/education/indicatoranalysis, www.help/prosperities/zigzag.htm.

The word "standard" in standard deviation refers to an annualized average. If a standard deviation is ±20 percent, it does not guarantee exactly a 20 percent rate of change. Over less than a year, the change can be much higher than the 20 percent average. Also, in any given year the rate of change can be much higher than 20 percent because 20 percent is only an average. Some years the rate of change will only be a few percent and some years it might be 30 percent. However, approximately five years per century a 10 percent target rate of return will experience a significantly greater rate of change than what is typical. Losses will be worse than 20 percent around five years per every one hundred years.

In practical terms, don't complain when your large cap stock portfolio with an expected rate of return of 10 percent a year has a decline of 20 percent. The negative 20 percent year is normal and is the price the investor pays to pursue a 10 percent return. Don't complain when a non-typical 30 percent loss occurs because, although rare, it is still normal.

All positive growth rates have a standard deviation or zigzag. As the expected rate of return increases so does the standard deviation.

The following tables illustrate the spectrum of the standard deviation that occurs as the expected rate of return changes for bonds and stocks.

Bonds

Type of Corporate Profit Received By the Investor	Expected Rate of Return	Standard Deviation or Zigzag Rate	Years to Recover
30 day corporate debt (bonds) commonly referred to as "money market"	1%	0	0
1 year corporate debt (bonds)	3%	5%	0
5 year corporate debt (bonds)	4%	7%	3
10 year corporate debt (bonds)	5%	8%	4
30 year corporate debt (bonds)	7%	11%	5

Stocks

Type of Corporate Profit Received By the Investor	Expected Rate of Return	Standard Deviation or Zigzag Rate	Years to Recover
Large corporate stocks	10%	20%	10
Smaller corporate stocks	12%	30%	15
Non U.S. stocks	14%	40%	?

The investor is free to choose whatever rate of return meets his long-term objectives. However, each rate of return has its own set of statistical consequences. An investor saving to build a house in two years does not want to attempt to earn a 10 percent rate of return. A 10 percent rate of return carries with it the inevitable consequence of having the very real potential of dropping in value 20 percent in any given year and it might take ten years to recover the principal.

A twenty-five- to fifty-five-year-old investing for retirement should have very little fear of a 20 percent decline that may take ten years to recover from because ten years is less than the number of years to retirement.

A twenty-five-year-old saving the value of a pack of cigarettes per day for forty years at a 10 percent average annualized return will accumulate $807,000. At a 3 percent rate of return the same amount saved grows to $137,000. It is irrational for a twenty-five-year-old to avoid the higher standard deviation and higher time of recovery when the time of recovery is a relatively short period versus the total number of expected years to work.

Fear of corporate profits is irrational. Society is corporate profits. All investments are 100 percent paid for by corporate profits and all markets are simply subsets or classifications of different statistical behavioral attributes (expected return, standard deviation, year to recovery) of corporate profits.

The investor should match the statistical attributes of a given expected rate of return to maximize the creation of wealth over x period of time.

Ironically, the lowest possible positive rate of return that has a zero standard deviation is the most dangerous long-term investment. The rate of return that has zero standard deviation is called the risk-free rate of return. The nickname "risk free" refers to its zero standard deviation statistical behavior (no zigzag). The problem with the risk-free rate is that it is a long-term loser. It seems like a positive rate of return—typically 1, 2, or 3 percent, (depending upon market conditions), but the positive number is an illusion. The risk-free rate of return minus taxes and inflation (theoretically) equals zero. In practice the risk-free return is actually a negative return. An investor who invests in a market which only yields the risk-free rate of return over a long period of time loses purchasing power. This problem is particularly evident with retirees who invest primarily in the risk-free marketplace. For example, the retiree needs $3000 per month to live so she invests to create approximately a $3000 per month income via the risk-free market. Then, ten years later it takes $4000 to buy the same lifestyle. But the retiree's income is still $3000. The investments were too safe. The zero standard deviation was misinterpreted as a desirable behavioral attribute. A rate of return with a zero standard deviation has no value; it is worthless. The risk-free rate of return is actually a negation of a real rate of return. An investor investing into a long-term negative return (the risk-free return) will fail to accumulate wealth.

A zero standard deviation should not be confused with storing a stack of currency in a lock box. Currency has a constant depreciation or constant decline in value, and, in addition does not earn any interest. In 1970 a new Volkswagon cost $1200. If an investor locked $1200 in a safety deposit box to store it for thirty years for the purpose of taking it out to buy a new car at retirement, then the investor is in for a bad surprise. The VW dealer sells the same car thirty years later for $20,000, not $1200. The car did not change in price; actually the car is cheaper to build in 2000 with robots versus the large labor force necessary in the 70s. The car did not change in value, the money did. The money shrunk by ten times over thirty years.[11]

The risk-free rate of return is the lowest possible rate of return in a capitalist society. It is impossible to earn less than the risk-free rate of return. That would imply a negative standard deviation, and a negative zigzag rate is impossible. A negative standard deviation, would be more quiet than absolute silence, or more still than absolute stillness: the laws of physics prohibit a negative standard deviation. The rate of return of the Social Security system is only one half the risk-free rate of return. By the laws of physics, the rate of return of the Social Security system is impossible. To calculate the Social Security rate of return, take the risk-free rate of return minus the government's hand in the cookie jar that equals a crime.

The investor must tolerate some ongoing zigzag rate to accumulate sufficient retirement assets. Some zigzag rate must be accepted to outpace inflation and taxes in order to create real gains. All returns on investments are paid for by corporate profits and corporate profits are not generated at an even pace.

---

[11]U.S. Department of Labor.

Reducing Risk through Mixing Assets

All positive rates of return have some corresponding level of standard deviation. As the rate of return increases, the level of zigzag also increases. And as standard deviation increases, the length of the market cycle increases. It is therefore in the investor's interest to maximize return while simultaneously minimizing the standard deviation.[12]

An expected 10 percent rate of return can have a wide range of associated standard deviation. A single stock or business can have an expected 10 percent growth rate. However, the risk or standard deviation of a single security can be 100 percent. An individual corporation can go out of business, completely failing, leaving the owner and lenders/stockholders and bondholders with a worthless security.

The investor's objective of 10 percent is a reasonable target; however, pursuing the target by investing in a single business is inefficient. The inefficiency occurs because it is possible to have a reasonable expectation of earning 10 percent over a long period of time without being exposed to the potential of a 100 percent loss. It is possible to earn 10 percent at considerably less standard deviation or volatility. Any investment's rate of return objective must also attempt to minimize volatility. Minimization of volatility accompanied by maximization of returns in a given marketplace is efficient. If either the minimization of risk or maximization of return fail to occur, then the exposure to the expected rate of return from corporate profit is inefficient. A participant in a 401(k) plan who intends to earn a 10 percent rate of return over thirty years will have extremely high odds of failure if he places 100 percent of his assets in a single stock. The odds of success are greatly improved by diversifying assets into more than one stock or bond. Two stocks have less risk and less return potential then a single stock. Even though a single stock has a higher return potential, the probability of success

---

[12]Mankowitz, Harry M. 1959 *Portfolio Selection: Efficient Diversification of Investments*. New York: John Wiley and Sons; Sharp, William F. 1970 *Portfolio Theory and Capital Markets*. New York: McGraw Hill.

is extremely remote, especially for the average investor. Another way of expressing improbability is inefficiency. Improbability is the potential of a high rate of return associated with an equally high likelihood of a 100 percent loss.[13]

The pension investor must reduce the risk to the point where the invested assets are most likely to meet the expected long-term rate of return objective. Volatility can be minimized through diversification; the greater the diversification, the greater the risk reduction (to a point). Short-term risk or volatility cannot be eliminated through diversification, it can only be minimized. It is better to minimize volatility than not, and diversification can eliminate the possibility of a 100 percent loss.

How much diversification is enough? The desired effect of diversification is to own enough businesses in a given industry so the aggregate behavior of the portfolio behaves similarly to the industry. If all large businesses in the U.S. economy generate an average 10 percent rate of return over a long period of time at a volatility rate of 20 percent then to behave similarly the investor must be diversified across all industry categories.

For example, the banking industry represents approximately 7 percent of the U.S. economy. Therefore, if an investor had a business objective to grow at a similar rate and with a similar risk in accordance with the 500 largest U.S. corporations, then the investor should be similarly weighted to each industry category. Thus, an approximate weighting of 7 percent in banking, and likewise a similar weighting in every category, would be necessary to achieve risk and return similar to the largest 500 domestic corporations.

Most stock money managers and stock mutual funds invest in eighty to a hundred different stocks. The industry weighting will depend upon the investment objective of the portfolio. There is a generally agreed upon mathematical principal which states that thirty samples within a universe should demonstrate behavior similar to the entire universe. Thirty stocks in an investment category should behave similarly to the category. The thirty stocks in the Dow Jones average should behave similarly to the S&P 500, and they do. The Dow 30 and S&P 500 are virtually identical in their rate of growth and rate of ups and downs.

All money comes from corporate profits. Corporate profits can be categorized in many classifications where the expected rate of return and

---

[13]"Central Limit Theorem," Published in *Business Statistics* by David F. Groebroe & Patrick W. Shannon, Columbus, OH: Merrill Publishing Co.

expected zigzag or volatility is accurately predictable over long periods of time. If the investor diversifies properly across a particular category then the investor can expect investment performance to be very similar to such a category.

A portfolio diversified throughout the technology sector should perform similarly to the sector. The expected rate of return of the sector is approximately 13 percent with an average zigzag rate of 40 percent.[14] If the volatility rate is too high for the investor, then the investor should not invest in the tech industry.

Each individual can choose any expected rate of return and its associated level of volatility with its corresponding time of recovery.

---

[14]Thomson Financial, *Investment View* (3/31/04), Rockville, MD.

Investment Categories

There are only two investment choices, either stocks (ownership of a corporation) or bonds (lending money to a corporation). Both investment choices' returns are 100 percent paid for through corporate profits. Within the choices of all possible stock or all possible bond classifications it is possible to create investment categories with specific anticipated statistical characteristics or specific expected zigzag rates and rate of return potential.

The categories are preset groupings of either corporate stock, or bonds, and sometimes both. The preset groupings or categories are designed in a variety of ways. There are categories based on physical commonality, such as groupings of big corporations, midsize and small. Categories can also be formulated based on the management philosophy of the corporation. For example, some corporate managers believe a consistent dividend is important. Corporations which consistently pay a dividend are then grouped into a dividend likely category.

Stock performance in large corporations has an expected rate of return of 10 to 12 percent and an expected volatility of 20 percent.[15] Small company stocks have a high expected rate of return, 15 percent, and therefore must also have a higher rate of volatility, approximately 35 percent. The investment categories are segmented to create discernable groups with clearly different expected risk and return categories. Typical categories are large companies, large companies which pay a dividend, midsize companies, small companies, foreign corporations, country-specific companies and industry-specific companies. Bonds are categorized for the same purpose. Debt is broken down into *years to maturity* and *credit quality.*

---

[15]Ibbotson and Associates, *SBBI 2003 Yearbook Market Results for 1926–2002: Stocks, Bonds, Bills, and Inflation.* Chicago: Ibbotson Associates.

For bonds, the *credit quality* expresses the likelihood the investor will be paid back, while *years to maturity* defines when the investor will be paid. Junk, or high yield bonds, have a generally more speculative nature, or a higher zigzag than bonds with a high credit rating.

Further categories of stock are statistically segmented by the methodology by which they are analyzed, or the style used by a manager to create a portfolio. A manager will declare the use of a particular style and the style will have particular predictable statistical characteristics. A portfolio of stocks for which the manager only buys stock that is expected to have higher than average earnings is called "growth." Another manager in the same category could buy stocks not for earning, but for the relative value of the stock price versus the sale price of the business. The value method and the growth method may be in the exact same category, but the two methods will behave differently.

These various categories have created the impression of many investment choices, when actually all the categories, styles, and methods are only a subset of corporate profits. The purpose of the various investment categories is to enable the investor to construct a diversified investment strategy by mixing the categories in such a fashion as to create any expected risk and return scenario. The rational investor can target any long-term wealth accumulation objective with an acceptable zigzag rate.

The Miracle of Mixing

T ouch a lit match to charcoal and there is a low probability of combustion. The same goes for sulfur or potassium nitrate. Combined as one, however, these three components create gunpowder. Touch the mixture of the three components with a lit match and the reaction is much different than that of the components individually. A mixture of three lowly combustible materials will behave differently than will each individual component. Gunpowder is highly combustible, but its individual components are not. The physics of chemistry is telling us that by mixing A, B, and C, the result is not a ratio of so much A and so much B, etc. The mixture creates something new, D, and D behaves differently then any of the ingredients behave alone.

Mixing investment categories can create a similar phenomenon in that the mixture of several categories can generate an entirely different effect than each individual category could. Investment A, which has a 20 percent volatility rate, and investment B, which has a 30 percent volatility rate, can together create a new expected volatility of 18 percent.[16] Reducing volatility can have significant practical applications.

Volatility minimization with simultaneous rate of return maximization is the definition of efficiency. This efficiency occurs when one investment category behaves differently than another. It is an additional step in the process of diversification, as the advantage of efficiency exceeds simply being spread over many stocks or bonds.

The S&P 500 is an index of the largest 500 domestic corporations. Spreading investments over the 500 largest domestic corporations solves several problems. It eliminates the risk of individual business failures affecting principal. The volatility rate will be similar to the aggregate stock market, it can never fail, and as long as society exists it will grow at the av-

---

[16]Markowitz, Harry M. 1959 *Portfolio Selection: Efficient Diversification of Investments.* New York: John Wiley and Sons; Sharp, William F. 1970 *Portfolio Theory and Capital Markets.* New York: McGraw Hill.

erage rate of corporate profits, around 10 percent.[17] The expected volatility of the S&P 500 is 20 percent up or 20 percent down on average in any given year with an expected growth rate of 10 percent.

The S&P 500 alone is, however, inefficient. It is inefficient because given the risk taken, in this example 20 percent (standard deviation), the financial markets offer a higher rate of return than the expected 10 percent. If an investor is willing to endure a 20 percent zigzag rate then the rate of return can be higher at no additional risk. Inefficiency is the state where at some level of volatility it is possible to earn more.

There are many investment categories, markets, and classifications capable of, when mixed together, creating a superior expected rate of return and expected volatility rate. The mixture can create a 12 percent return at 20 percent risk, which is better than a 10 percent return at 20 percent risk. There is a point when efficiency is reached and improvements are no longer possible. The S&P 500 is less than efficient because many other mixtures are superior.[18]

The practical application of diversification for the typical 401(k) investor is to be diversified into many individual securities and additionally be diversified in efficient mixes of various market categories, markets, and classifications. Only a mixture of investment categories, markets, and classifications can achieve efficiency. A single category, market, or classification is always inefficient.

This means the investor must first be diversified within markets such as small cap domestic stocks, for example, and second, be further diversified in various markets. Third, the various markets cannot be just any markets, they must feature non-correlating relationships.[19] The mix of markets is most efficient when a given economic stimulus X occurs, and as a result of the stimulus some markets move up and some move down. Economic event X could be a rise in interest rates. In reaction to the change of rates, the desired effect of seven different markets, categories, and classifications would be to have some go up, some go down, and some go sideways. The efficiency becomes maximized as the differing behaviors of the multiple markets are least correlated or act differently to a significant degree.

---

[17]Department of Commerce.
[18]Markowitz, Harry M. 1959 *Portfolio Selection: Efficient Diversification of Investments*. New York: John Wiley and Sons.
[19]Markowitz, Harry M. 1959 *Portfolio Selection: Efficient Diversification of Investments*. New York: John Wiley and Sons.

Retirees who invest 100 percent of their assets in debt or bonds do so not because they are consciously pursuing a low rate of return, but because they are primarily seeking low volatility—perceived low risk. The consequence of low volatility is low return, which in time may lessen an investment's purchasing power. The loss of purchasing power is a risk, unforeseen but still a potent force of danger for the retired.

By mixing both low standard deviation bonds and higher standard deviation stocks, at certain values, it is possible to match the low standard deviation of bonds while simultaneously increasing the rate of return. This mixture creates a high enough return to forever keep pace with inflation and never lose purchasing power. This solution exists because a portfolio of 100 percent bonds is inefficient. Bonds alone cannot simultaneously maximize both risk and return. No single market can be efficient. There is room to increase the rate of return without increasing risk in this example because a single market is inefficient. A diversified bond portfolio only satisfies part of the total diversification solution. Multimarkets are still necessary to maximize a rate of return and minimize the amount of risk.

There is nothing wrong with the retiree's objective of low risk as long as the aggregate portfolio is efficient (multimarket).

Mixing gold, silver, and platinum does not produce any benefits of diversification because all these markets move in concert with each other; if one is up, then all go up, and vice versa. Practical diversification occurs when investment categories move in opposing directions. For example, real estate stocks increase as interest rates rise as growth stocks typically decline.

Don't Buy and Sell

W hat is it about investing which fosters the delusional thinking of the lay person to believe outperforming the professional is routinely possible? There are approximately 500 people in the United States out of 280 million who can generate a consistent above-market (whatever market) return. Their income starts in the $5 million range and goes up to $100 million-plus. Most of the 500 have very large organizations with research budgets of many millions or even hundreds of millions behind them.

The error in overestimating one's skills is caused by both the length of the business cycle and the propensity of various investment classes to have four-, five-, or seven-year cycles.[20]

Ronald Reagan lowered federal taxes in 1980 from 70 percent to 26 percent, setting off a twenty-year bull market. Prior to 1980, under Jimmy Carter, a person making $5 million per year took home $500,000, enough to live with some frills. Suddenly, under Reagan, the $500,000 take-home pay moved to $3.7 million per year. This capital went flying into the market (corporate activity), flushing business with more capital, and generating very favorable business conditions. Even Joseph Stalin would have to admit moving the tax rate from 70 percent to 26 percent would stimulate the economy. Coincidentally, communism failed shortly after Reagan reduced taxes—something about communism's inability to compete.

The resulting twenty-year up cycle enabled domestic large capitalized stocks (big companies) to generate strong, consistent returns. During this period almost every stock increased in value. Certain industry categories such as technology and finance were seemingly always out performing their respective target because these markets had five- to seven-year periods of good performance without any negative yearly losses. Investors were

---

[20]"Business Cycle Expansions and Contractions." National Bureau of Economics, July 17, 2003. www.nber.org/cycles.html.

swimming with the current and erroneously attributed their rate of return to *a priori* skill.

The pension investor must establish an objective and investment strategy for many decades that cannot fail. Failure means loss of retirement. A single error can destroy a lifetime of savings. Chasing a four-year market category upcycle is certain failure. The more a market upcycle is pursued, and the more assets invested in a run up, the greater the loss to principal when the upcycle inevitably ends.

Don't draw to an inside straight because the odds are against the gambler. Sometimes novice gamblers in a single instance may win by drawing to an inside straight. However, engaging in a continuous behavior pattern against the odds has a certain outcome: loss.

A thousand individual thirty-seven-year-old investors buy ten stocks and hold the stocks for seven years. What is the outcome? Approximately 20 percent will exceed the typical benchmarks (give or take 5 percent) and 80 percent will not. The 10 to 20 percent who win the game for seven years are doomed to play it again for the next seven years and the next seven years and the next seven years. They must continue engaging in a low-probability game repeatedly until age sixty-five. The more they play, the worse the odds.

What happens to investors who risk their life savings over a twenty- to thirty-year period? Over the first seven years, 20 percent win and 80 percent do not. Of the one thousand who started out with high hopes, two hundred are left. Then comes the next seven years. Of the two hundred winners, one hundred sixty lose and forty win. Of the forty remaining winners during the next seven years, only eight remain winners. That is, out of one thousand investors, eight survive over twenty-one years, or, to put it in mathematical terms, eight divided by a thousand equals eight tenths of one percent (.008).

The surest method of success is to buy and hold mutual funds over long periods of time. If a thousand investors use this method then a thousand win.

A major mutual fund company may have a trillion dollars under management, and a research budget of $400 million that has three to four hundred top-tier analysts. The company receives twenty-two thousand applications from business school graduates and only hires fifteen to twenty per year. After ten years of apprenticeship the analyst can actually become a fund manager. Still the fund manager chooses her stock from those the four hundred very bright analysts have analyzed. When an analyst decides to sell an auto stock the analyst must know all auto companies, have visited all auto companies, know all the business which supply and support the auto industry, and do this globally. When General Electric states they will make a profit in the power business in China, the analyst goes to China, reviews all

GE energy contracts globally, then reviews all GE's competitors in China and globally, reviews the energy industry globally and then decides whether GE is telling the truth or not with the extra advantage of having personal access to GE executives.

How is a surgeon with ten minutes free time per week going to achieve the same type of in-depth market knowledge? How could a steel worker or anyone match the research done on a $100 million research budget? As analysts move through their careers and become managers, managers grow old, retire, and are replaced with other experienced, well-trained analysts. Consistent performance is maintained by a large mutual fund via a constant flow of knowledgeable employees.

Corporations are interrelated in many different ways and to make a single transaction the investor must know everything there is to know about many industries, how the industries relate, and who all the players are.

Buying and selling mutual funds makes less sense than buying and selling individual securities. The investor does not know what securities are in a fund at any given time. Mutual fund companies disclose a sample of what was in their portfolios several months in the past. Therefore, the investor does not know which stocks were sold and which stocks were purchased in the intervening months. Even if the investor did have an accurate list of securities, what good would it do? Who has the time to analyze a list of one hundred stocks to buy and one hundred to sell? It would take an individual years to do what a mutual fund can do in one day. By the time an individual arrived at the correct answer the world would have changed and the answer would no longer apply.

Fidelity Investments did a study that discovered there were differences between their funds' performance and their clients' performance. One of their funds earned an average rate of return of 15 percent for twenty years while the investors who owned the fund only earned 6 percent. After reviewing their records, it was discovered the average investor only held the fund for eleven months. The investor was jumping in and out and as a consequence, destroyed their long-term rate of return. If the investor would have simply remained in the fund and let the professional manager— backed by a $400 million research budget—do her job, then the investor would have earned 15 percent per year, not 6 percent.

Over the past ten years, or twenty-five hundred trading days, the domestic market average (S&P 500) earned an annual average rate of return of 12 percent. If the best forty rate-of-return days are subtracted from the twenty-five hundred, the rate of return drops to −0.5 percent. During ten years of investing, which generated a compound average annualized rate of return of 12 percent, if the investor missed only forty business days of market gains, the $+12$ percent per year would have been reduced to a negative -0.5 percent per year.

The odds of buying and selling stock and hitting the current up day are approximately 16 in one thousand. The buyer and seller are then playing a game where the odds of success are greatly against winning. Put a thousand marbles in a jar: 984 black and 16 white. Shake the jar to randomly distribute the black and white marbles. Blindfolded, reach into the jar and choose a marble. See and record the color of the marble, put it back and repeat the process twenty times. See how many white marbles were chosen: likely zero. Pension plans, 401(k)s and profit sharing plans are your life savings. Don't lose all your marbles by buying and selling.

The long-term rate of return of corporate profits over a pensioner's lifetime is likely to be in the 10 percent range. Every time a buy or sell decision is interjected into the equation the odds of achieving the expected 10 percent decline. It is the same as multiplying 10 percent by $1/x$, a number less than a whole number. The fraction $1/x$ is used because the probability of a guess cannot equal one because it is impossible to know the future and anyone's best guess is a subset of reality. Therefore a best guess is a fraction—a less than whole number. In this case, reality is the long-term rate of growth of corporate profits, and the buy or sell decision reduces the probability of obtaining the expected 10 percent rate of return. What happens when our investor makes ten buy and sells? $(1/x) \times (1/x) \times (1/x) =$ one over x to the tenth power (a very small probability). Regardless of what x actually equals, the investor loses because 10 percent is lessened. Don't buy and sell.

The odds of meeting long-term rate of return objectives improve as one holds an array of good mutual funds. See the table below:

Five-year returns of a sample of large mutual fund companies and their relative returns versus the S&P 500 index.

Putnam	80% of stock funds outperformed the S&P 500
Fidelity	80% of stock funds outperformed the S&P 500
Oppenheimer	90% of stock funds outperformed the S&P 500
American Funds	90% of stock funds outperformed the S&P 500
Franklin	80% of stock funds outperformed the S&P 500
Strong	70% of stock funds outperformed the S&P 500
Janus	80% of stock funds outperformed the S&P 500
All stock funds	70% of stock funds outperformed the S&P 500
Funds exceeding 10%	92% of stock funds outperformed 10% per year

As of 3/31/04 (Investment View) Thomson Financial data of stock funds with a portfolio of at least 80% in stock or more

Through the trailing five years ending the first quarter of 2004, a sample of large mutual fund companies a largely outperformed the S&P 500 index.

The best strategy is to place money into a large mutual fund and hold the fund for many years.

There is only one known historical record of any human ever being able to predict when a given market would go up, down, or sideways. If such a skill were possible the person who possessed it would shortly control the world as Pharaoh did many years ago.

The Biblical Joseph correctly predicted a fourteen year grain cycle in Egypt 4000 years ago. Joseph, who had a prison record, quickly became the second most powerful man on earth, second only to Pharaoh. However, Joseph had an edge—he spoke directly with God. Other than the team of Joseph and Pharaoh, no other human has been able to completely and accurately time any market. If anyone could, the evidence shows that such a person would become world ruler.

The short-term behavior of markets is random. Randomness cannot be mathematically predicted. Without mathematical predictability, foretelling short-term market behavior is truly impossible.

For something to be true it must be observable. If timing the market were possible then those who timed it could be observed. If a $10 million pension plan in 1926 was managed by a successful market timer then it would be worth over $18 trillion today by timing the markets just once per year. There is not $18 trillion on earth, let alone in someone's pension plan.

If someone could time the markets, then why not do it daily? It would then take about fifteen years for someone who was capable of timing the markets on a daily basis to accumulate all of the world's capital. This has not been observed.

Money managers outperform the market averages because they spend a lot of resources analyzing stocks, one by one, industry by industry, and economy by economy. Managers do not time the market.

Index

There are approximately fifteen thousand publicly traded corporations in the United States. The investing public is free to purchase ownership or lend money to any business which is publicly traded. Investors need to know what the future expected behavior of their investments will be. If a dollar is invested, how fast will it grow? What is the expected standard deviation? How much diversification is sufficient to eliminate the risk of a total loss? And what amount of time can the investment be down in value before it recovers?

To answer investor questions regarding investment rate of return expectations, a system of behavioral identification, is possible by creating a grouping of like categories of corporations. This system of behavioral identification has evolved beginning with Dow Jones's 11-stock sample of large railroad companies in 1884, and has moved to today's list of hundreds of preset stock or bond groupings. These preset groupings of stocks are called indices. An index is a specific preset group of stocks or bonds which is designed to be reflective of a given market category.

For example, what would an investor expect the future rate of return, standard deviation, and time to recover be of an investment in large U.S. corporate stock? The answer is estimated by reviewing the behavior of a variety of preset large stock groupings or indices. An appropriate indicator of large corporation investment return behaviors is the Dow Jones industrial average, which is comprised of thirty large corporations in various key industries. Several large corporate indices such as the Russell top 200, the S&P 400, the S&P 500 or Russell 1000 all reveal the statistical attributes of a diversified group of U.S. large cap corporate investment behavior.

There are a variety of indices for every imaginable segment of the fifteen thousand publicly traded corporations. A portfolio concentrated in smaller corporations can be compared to the Russell 3000, the S&P small cap 600, the Thompson small cap mutual funds, the Wilshire 5000, and so on. There is an index for every industry type such as real estate, utilities, technology, transportation, energy, and health care. There are also indices reflective of manager styles, such as growth, value, asset allocation, income, and trend. Portfolios which mix both stocks and bonds even have comparison indices. For every Jack there is a Jill, for every type of portfolio there is a reflective preset grouping of stocks or bonds expressed as an index.

Therefore, an index is a tool used to estimate the investment return behavior of a given subset of these fifteen thousand publicly traded corporations. No matter how the investor segments the market of all possible securities, it is possible to find a preset grouping (index) of stocks or bonds to match the given segment. The practical application of an index is to enable the investor to foretell the long-term expected rate of return. By accurately estimating the long-term return, the investor increases the likelihood of meeting his wealth accumulation objective. An index is also used as a barometer to see if the management of the assets is behaving as it should. A portfolio of large cap stocks using the value style should perform similarly to the Barra large cap value index. The concept is simple. Match the index to the portfolio characteristics. Use the index as a tool to predict future behavior, use it to measure performance in the present and use it to look backward into the past to compare actual returns with expected returns. Therefore, an index is a preset grouping of securities, either stocks or bonds, used to predict an investment's behavior, measure investment performance by comparing the actual results to an index with similar characteristics, and as a long-term planning tool.

If the S&P 500 (largest 500 U.S. corporations) index has an expected standard deviation of 20 percent with an expected rate or return of 10 percent and a worst-case recovery period of ten years, then an investor can estimate with a high degree of accuracy a generally successful large mutual fund invested in similar corporations will experience similar investment behavior.

The following table lists the investment subset of fifteen thousand corporations, either ownership (stock) or debt (bonds), with the expected standard deviation and expected rate of return.

Investment Subset	Annualized Volatility or Standard Deviations	Expected Returns	Examples of a Measuring Index
Cash	0	2%	30 day money market/Merrill Lynch 91 day
Short-term bonds	3	4%	LB Intermediate

Investment Subset	Annualized Volatility or Standard Deviations	Expected Returns	Examples of a Measuring Index
10 year bonds	5	6%	Solomon Brothers Corporate Bonds
Long-term bonds	8	7%	LB Long Corporate
Balanced funds	12	8%	Wiesenberger Balanced Domestic/S&P 60%, LB 40%
Dividend stocks	15	9%	BARRA value
Large cap stocks	20	10%	S&P 500
Mid cap stocks	25	11%	Russell mid cap S&P mid cap
Foreign stocks	30	12%	EAFAE
Small cap stock	35	13%	Russell 2000 Russell 3000

Each investment category subset has a corresponding index to measure investments' expected behavior. Indices have become very common; so common in fact that marketers of investments have packaged the index into mutual funds which are marketed on the premise of average returns, average risk, and low cost. The actual results of index funds versus managed funds place the index performance at the bottom of the pack. An index is not an average, it is a preset list of corporations; good ones, bad ones, and in some cases, very bad ones.

An Index Used as an Investment Rather than a Measuring Tool

Somewhere deep within the creative minds of Wall Street, some bright sales executive thought selling a measuring device as a packaged product would be a good idea. That is, sell an index as an investment package.

An index is a measurement tool comprised of a predetermined list of securities. As the securities in an index are simply a preset list of stocks or bonds without regard to quality, there is consequently no cost of analysis. The S&P 500 index (for example) is made up simply of the 500 largest U.S. corporations. Selling a preset list of securities avoids the expense of a manager deciding which corporation has an expected high growth rate, not buying corporations which have an expected poor growth rate and selling corporations which once had a high growth rate but no longer do. The highly paid analysts who visit corporations, read financial information and discuss the future prospects of corporate profits with management are also avoided. Between the manager, team of analysts and their support staff, at least half of a percent worth of expenses can be avoided.

The average cost of asset management for a typical mutual fund is approximately 1 percent of assets. By avoiding the costs of skilled management, an index of stocks can be sold for 0.4 to 0.5 percent in total costs. The selling concept of an index fund is "cheaper is better." The seller has low expenses and high profit margins and the rate of return should always be average, in theory. The index product can be sold by an uneducated workforce because there is not any analysis required. Putting a worker's life savings into a preset list of corporations requires very little skill.

The problem is, indices do not have average performance. The hard evidence does not support the viability of index performance. An index typically underperforms a similar group of managers and/or mutual funds. A preset list of securities includes both productive and unproductive businesses. The list will include the industries of the future as well as those that have been all but invented out of business. A preset list includes all conditions, both good and bad. Also, the very existence of a preset list of corporations having money blindly dumped into it does not allow the marketplace to suppress or weed out the inefficient businesses while simultaneously rewarding the efficient.

First consider the hard evidence of the performance of the S&P 500 versus a universe of stock mutual fund managers. The sellers of the S&P 500 index will use sales tactics which create a statistically improperly designed universe of mutual fund mangers to compare performance. Their argument is, the index outperforms x percent of mutual funds. Typically "a majority," they say. The problem is, the construct of the universe of mutual fund managers unrealistically excludes most of the mutual fund industry. Fidelity Investments is the largest mutual fund manger and Fidelity funds are typically excluded from the comparison universe the index sellers use. How can an objective mutual fund universe which is used for comparison purposes exclude the largest mutual fund manager? That would be like analyzing the discount retail industry, but excluding WalMart from the study. What value would a study of the discount retail industry have if the largest discount merchandiser were excluded? What value for analytical comparison purposes does the universe of mutual fund managers have if the largest fund manager is excluded? Fidelity is not the only major mutual fund excluded, there are more.

The trick used by the sellers of index funds is to construct a comparison universe which the index fund outperforms. The trick is to create a list of mutual funds with a very similar investment strategy and underlying portfolio such as the S&P 500 Index. At first glance this seems perfectly logical: compare apples to apples. The problem is, very few mutual fund managers limit their strategy to the S&P 500. Refer back to page 60 on why a single index is inefficient. Only a mixture of markets can be efficient and any individual market is always inefficient. The S&P 500 is an individual market and alone it is inefficient. To be efficient (maximize return and minimize risk) the S&P 500 must be mixed with other markets.

Mutual fund managers are certainly aware of the benefits of creating efficiencies through diversification. Most mutual fund managers do not limit their funds to a single market. The prevalent mutual fund management methodology is contradictory to the narrow definition used by the sellers of index funds. Of course, the sellers of index funds know this, as their use of improperly constructed universes is by intent.

By defining a comparison universe more inclusively to capture more accurately the typical mutual fund, the performance relationship between managed assets and a preset list of securities dramatically changes.

The following set of graphs explains how to read mutual fund returns and how a universe of mutual funds can be compared to an index.

View a mutual fund as a dot with yet to be defined coordinates:
- (x,y)

Add a rate of return coordinate when y = 10%.

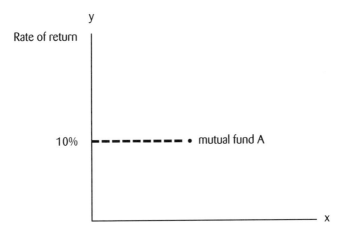

Add the standard deviation coordinate x = 20%.

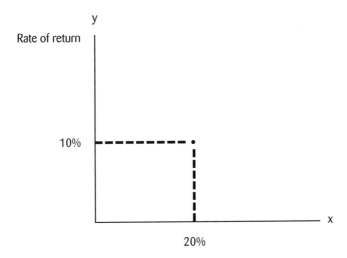

The above graph illustrates mutual fund A has earned 10 percent with a 20 percent standard deviation over Z amount of time. Time is reflected in the risk and return as long-term averages.

Add time where z = 10 years.

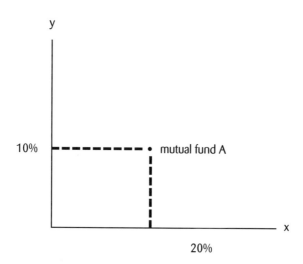

Now mutual fund A earned an average annualized rate of return of 10 percent with a 20 percent standard deviation over 10 years of time.
Observe the difference between mutual fund A and mutual fund B.

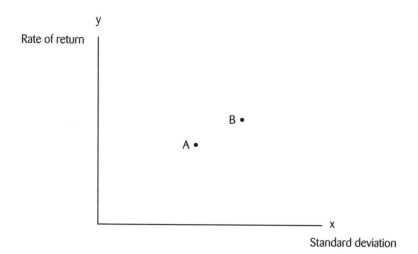

Mutual fund B has a higher rate of return than mutual fund A.

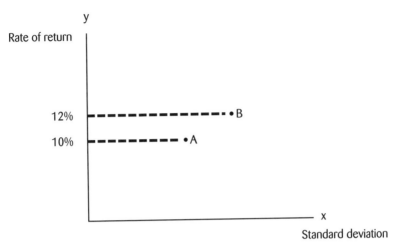

AVERAGE RISK AND RETURN OVER TEN YEARS

Mutual fund B earned an average annualized rate of return of 12 percent per year for 10 years and mutual fund A earned less at 10 percent. Compare the risk of mutual fund A to mutual fund B.

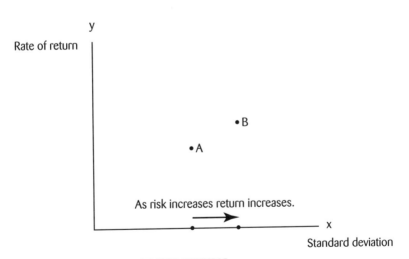

TEN YEARS AVERAGE RISK AND RETURN

Mutual fund B has more risk, or a higher standard deviation.

Mutual fund B has a higher standard deviation than mutual fund A.

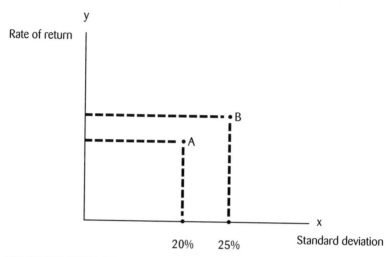

TEN YEARS AVERAGE RISK AND RETURN

Mutual fund A has a return and risk coordinate of 10 percent, 20 percent over 10 years and mutual fund B has a return and risk coordinate of 12 percent, 25 percent. It is possible to quickly see mutual fund B over 10 years has both a higher standard deviation and rate of return than mutual fund A.

Over the past five years, mutual fund stock managers who are at least 80 percent invested in stocks have outperformed their respective index, the S&P 500. The following two graphs plot 5,733 stock funds with a one-year history (the trailing twelve months through the first quarter of 2004) and 4,238 stock funds with a five-year history (five years through the first quarter of 2004). Both graphs clearly reveal the vast majority of funds outperforming their index. The index is represented as the solid black circle at the intersection of the vertical and horizontal dotted lines. Each lighter circle which is above, or north of, the solid black circle is outperforming the benchmark index (S&P 500). It is immediately clear that 80 percent of the lighter circles are above (outperform) the black circle.

The next two graphs plot the performance of bond mutual funds with the comparative index as the Lehman Brother Credit Bond. These graphs follow the same schematics as the stock mutual graphs except they illustrate a universe of bond funds compared to a bond index. In these examples, the typical bond manager is beneath or under the index which depicts the majority of bond managers as underperforming. Bond managers know the

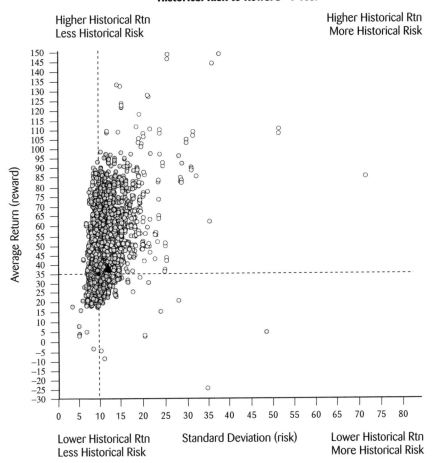

Historical Risk to Reward–1 Year

Higher Historical Rtn
Less Historical Risk

Higher Historical Rtn
More Historical Risk

Average Return (reward)

Lower Historical Rtn
Less Historical Risk

Standard Deviation (risk)

Lower Historical Rtn
More Historical Risk

bond market is poised for a strong decline and therefore are avoiding risk in the present to protect their investors' money in the future.

The evidence, as depicted on the preceding graphs and developed from Thomson Financial data, clearly illustrates how stock mutual funds can outperform the S&P 500 index. Of the major firms—Fidelity, American Funds, Franklin, Putnam, and Oppenheimer—over 88 percent of their stock funds outperformed the S&P 500 index. Conversely, as in the bond example, outperforming the index might create a bad long-term result for the investor.

The superior performance of mutual funds versus the S&P 500 index is caused by the diversification advantages of the managed funds because

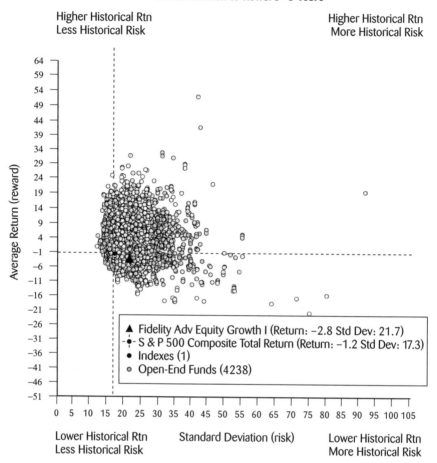

Historical Risk to Reward—5 Years

Higher Historical Rtn
Less Historical Risk

Higher Historical Rtn
More Historical Risk

Average Return (reward)

▲ Fidelity Adv Equity Growth I (Return: −2.8 Std Dev: 21.7)
- ● - S & P 500 Composite Total Return (Return: −1.2 Std Dev: 17.3)
● Indexes (1)
○ Open-End Funds (4238)

Lower Historical Rtn
Less Historical Risk

Standard Deviation (risk)

Lower Historical Rtn
More Historical Risk

an index, representing a single market, is inefficient when compared to a mixture of markets. Also, a preset list of stocks or bonds has both obvious winners and losers. A mutual fund manager can look past the immediate daily fluctuation in stock prices toward the long-term viability of a business. The Pony Express and the telegraph existed at the same time. One business sent messengers at an average speed of ten miles per hour at great expense and the other sent messages at the speed of light almost cost free. Horse-drawn and horseless carriages existed at the same time; which one had a future and which was headed for the museum? Over time managers

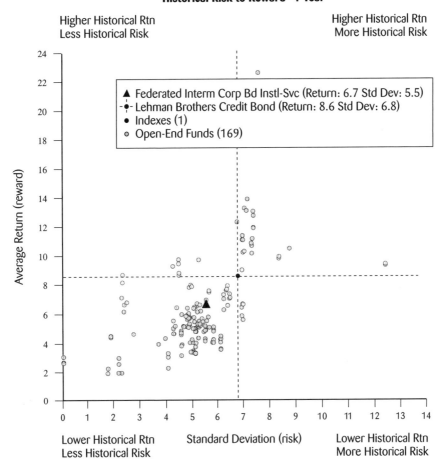

Historical Risk to Reward—1 Year

Higher Historical Rtn
Less Historical Risk

Higher Historical Rtn
More Historical Risk

▲ Federated Interm Corp Bd Instl-Svc (Return: 6.7 Std Dev: 5.5)
-●- Lehman Brothers Credit Bond (Return: 8.6 Std Dev: 6.8)
● Indexes (1)
○ Open-End Funds (169)

Average Return (reward)

Standard Deviation (risk)

Lower Historical Rtn
Less Historical Risk

Lower Historical Rtn
More Historical Risk

can weed out the future winners and losers better than a preset list of securities can; but it takes time to show up in the performance.

The very fact of an index being sold to the public as an investment creates trouble in the financial markets. Normally, if a business is either on the ball or sloppy, the marketplace would provide either reward or punishment.

Managers protect investors by avoiding obvious problem stocks.

A business being poorly operated, dishonest, or invented out of business would have its stock prices lowered by the analysis of skilled managers. The managers would see to it that a factory worker's hard-earned

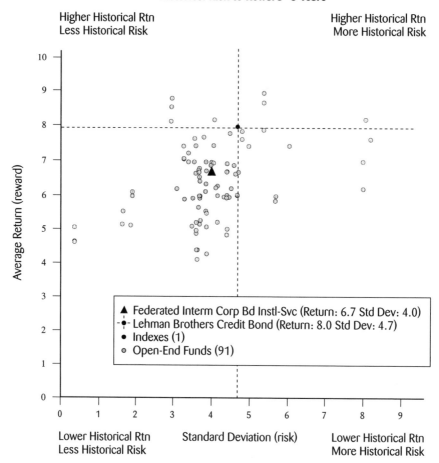

Historical Risk to Reward–5 Years

life savings were not being deposited into a soon to be or presently bankrupt business. An index blindly buys into a preset list regardless of the future viability of the businesses. This means the hard-earned assets of a person depositing money into an index is intentionally being invested into known losers.

To make matters worse, as the index is weighted due to size, if the corporation dishonestly inflates its earnings it will cause the index to buy more. Dishonesty is rewarded under the index system when it should be punished under normal market conditions. The example of Enron illustrates this issue. Enron became one of the top purchases of the S&P 500 index. The more Enron lied about its earnings the more the index purchased its stock. Eventually Enron's misbehavior was uncovered and the company went bankrupt. Even bankrupt and exposed as totally corrupt, Enron stock remained in the S&P 500 index. This means a hard-working steel worker in Somewhereville, Pennsylvania who had an index fund in his or her 401(k) plan was knowingly dumping precious retirement funds into a worthless stock. A total waste of hard sweat-earned money. Not only do index funds underperform the typical mutual fund, they also rigidly deposit assets into known failed and/or failing businesses.

During the strong bull (overpriced) market of the 1990s, stock became clearly overvalued. Mutual fund managers began to shy away from the market runup and reduced their holdings in overpriced stocks. The index, on the other hand, increased its purchases of the overvalued stocks. The higher the overvaluation, the more the index purchased. The index is blind—the higher the stock price becomes the more it is purchased. This is essentially the opposite of what the investor should do.

Indices, if used at all as investment vehicles, should be purchased sparingly.

There are periods of time when the index will be above the majority of funds. This does not mean the managers are falling behind the index. It means the stocks or bonds in the index have been blindly purchased to the extent which prudent managers would refuse to buy overpriced securities on behalf of their clients. The manager exercises judgement and avoids an overpriced market even though an overpriced market may have a bubble before it inevitably pops and the index investor incurs big losses. Good money deposited into an overvalued index will cause overvalued stocks to become more overvalued as the index blindly purchases securities regardless of their true underlying value or future commercial prospects.

If index funds were available in 1860, then the hard-earned money of American workers who used index funds for their retirement savings would have been buying Pony Express stock. The 1860 index fund would have blindly purchased Pony Express stock even as the telegraph wires were being strung. Investing in the Pony Express was a waste of money, but an index fund would have poured money into the failed concept.

This is currently happening in the bond market. As interest rates increase, bonds decrease. Bond managers are avoiding bonds, which is temporarily causing the average bond manager to underperform the bond index. The bond managers are avoiding the obvious pitfalls of a rising rate environment and protecting their clients, but as a result, the managers are underperforming the bond index.

Taxes

Taxes are part of investing. Future gains are constantly being suppressed by taxes, so by avoiding taxes, legally, it will improve the investor's long-term rate of return. To review how the typical American is taxed it is helpful to review how taxes reduce wealth in the hunting village.

The hunting village obtains 100 percent of its food, clothing, and shelter from the proceeds of the hunt. There is not any other way any member of the village can survive other than from the proceeds of the hunt. To maintain social order, the village establishes a chief, who presides over social stability. Being chief is a non-hunting occupation so the chief must tax the hunting party enough meat to feed himself and his family and tax the hunters their deer by-products for clothing and shelter.

Each member of the village has less meat due to the amount that was given to the chief. If the annual meat production was one thousand pounds and the chief took eight hundred pounds then there is two hundred pounds remaining to be distributed to the villagers. The chief took approximately 80 percent of the villager's wealth.

All wealth of the hunting village is created from the proceeds of the hunting party.

Activity of the
hunting party
which is producing
deer for the village

This activity represents 100 percent of the source of wealth of the hunting village.

From the activity of the hunting party, which of course is hunting, meat and deer by-products are produced. The portion of the production that is in excess of the internal needs of the hunting party is the hunting profit.

If the hunting party needed to hunt for two weeks to produce one hundred pounds of meat and the members of the hunting party found it necessary to eat ten pounds during their hunt, then the remaining ninety pounds is the gross profit, which is the wealth created for the village.

The gross profit is measured and determined to be ninety pounds. The chief would then print ninety one-dollar bills with each bill representing one actual pound of meat.

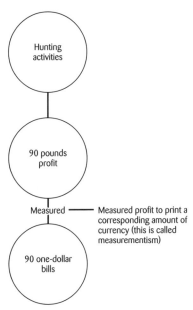

The act of measuring the gross profit of the hunting party (meat) and printing a corresponding amount of currency is called measurementism. Using measurementism, the hunting party generates ninety pounds of profit. Then, the ninety pounds are measured, and ninety one-dollar bills are created. A villager can have some comfort in the true value of the one-dollar bill being actually one pound of meat because the profits were measured. Then if a villager would like to purchase a spear from her neighbor and the spear is worth ten real pounds of meat, both the buyer and seller will feel comfortable using ten dollars to make the transaction. Using real meat would not be necessary as the currency is actually worth a corresponding amount of meat. The currency is worth a corresponding amount of meat because it was actually measured as such.

The wealth created by the hunting party in the form of gross profit is not the wealth the villager receives. If there are ninety villagers and there are ninety pounds of meat wealth created, then each villager gained one pound in wealth before taxes.

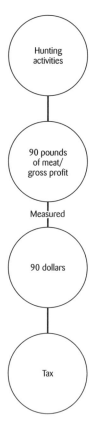

The ninety dollars in created wealth is taxed at a 50 percent corporate tax rate before the villagers receive their share. The first deduction from the villagers' wealth is the corporate tax.

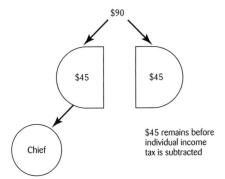

Forty-five dollars is deducted from gross profit due to the corporate tax rate. The villagers must pay the corporate tax indirectly because it reduces the wealth of each individual.

Half of the $90 or $45 goes to the chief.

The remaining $45 is cut in half again by individual income taxes. This means another $22.50 is sent to the chief.

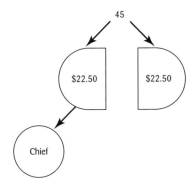

Therefore the villagers' wealth is reduced by both the corporate and the individual tax.

The villagers then receive their portion of the wealth created by the hunting party. Instead of receiving $1.00 each, the villagers receive roughly $0.225. That is, 77.5 percent of their wealth was taken by the chief.

The chief puts 77.5 percent of the village's wealth in his own pocket without the villager realizing what happened. The chief tells the villager the hunting party is mean and greedy and deserves a 50 percent tax rate. The villagers believe this because in a preindustrial hunting village the villager's brain apparently has not developed enough to understand taxing the hunting party is the same as taxing each villager.

The villager takes $0.225 and spends it, but can only buy $0.20 worth of goods because of sales tax.

Taxes in the Modern World

A ll wealth is created from corporate activity; there is not any other source of wealth. Corporate activity generates wealth in excess of the internal expenses of the corporation. This excess is corporate profit.

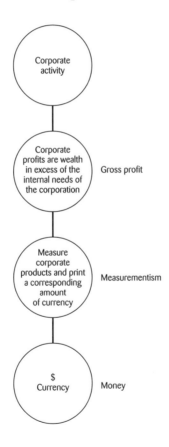

Corporate profits are measured and a corresponding amount of currency is printed. The value of the currency is actually equal to the value of products produced.

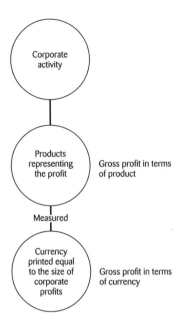

The profit of corporations is measured and is accounted for in units of currency. The gross profit is transformed into currency and taxed before it is recaptured by the workers, managers, and whoever created it.

If a steelworker (worker #1) created $200,000 worth of wealth, the worker is paid in the following manner:

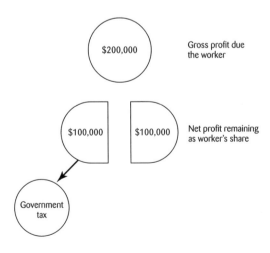

Worker #1 receives half of his share due to income tax.

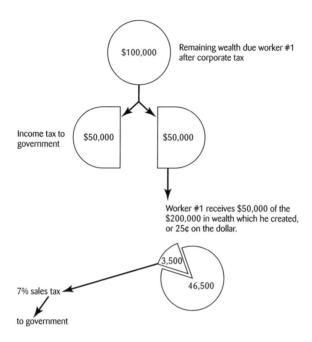

More tax is taken via state, local, and real estate taxes.

A steelworker who receives a salary of $46,500 actually earned $200,000. The worker kept 23 percent of the wealth created by his effort. The worker is told taxing the corporation is a good idea because the corporation is mean and greedy.

To retire, the worker must save some money. The best method to save is through a 401(k) plan because the amount saved is put into the plan before it is taxed. By avoiding the income tax the worker keeps 50 percent of his money as opposed to only keeping 23 percent.

Inflation

A ll wealth is created through corporate profits. There is not any other source of wealth.

All wealth is derived from corporate activity.
Corporations produce in excess of their internal needs.

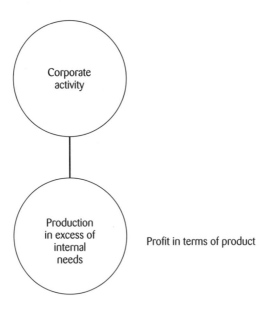

Profit in terms of product

The profit in terms of a product is transformed by measurement into currency.

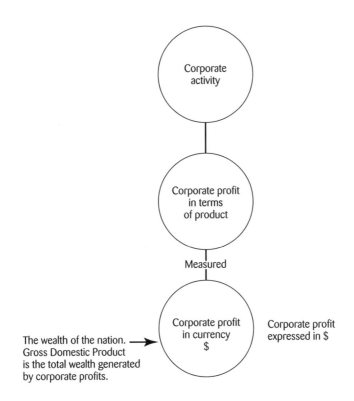

Corporate profits expressed in dollars are created by measuring every piece of steel, wheat, plastic, paint, finished product, effort, thought, etc. and re-expressing products into currency so the currency actually represents the real value of the products created. Therefore, a dollar is in reality a little piece of every product produced. Then a steelworker who purchases groceries worth eight hundred pounds of steel can give the grocer currency, as opposed to dropping an eight hundred pound piece of steel on the checkout counter. The grocer will feel confident the currency is really worth eight hundred pounds of steel and accept the currency as opposed to demanding the actual eight hundred pounds of steel.

The relationship between the amount of currency printed and the actual production of corporate profits must be accurate and honest or society will financially fail. The currency must truly represent the real value of production or the citizens will lose trust in the currency.

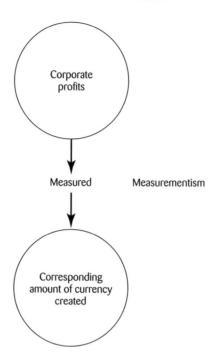

Measured   Measurementism

The trustworthiness of the money is assured through the simple act of measuring the products and only printing currency relative to the actual goods and services produced. This act of measuring is called measurementism.

The financial system operates as follows:

Step 1—Corporate activity is a business doing whatever it does.

Step 2—The business generates wealth in excess of its internal operating expenses. This wealth is called profit.

Step 3—The profit created by the goods or services is redefined into currency by measuring the profit and printing a corresponding amount of currency. This is the process of measurementism.

Step 4—Once the currency is created most of it is taken by the government (sub step 5). First 50 percent is taken via corporate tax and the remaining half is taxed again as income tax by another 50 percent. The remaining 25 percent of the wealth created by the corporations is paid to the workers and owners.

Step 5—The workers and owners receive their portion of the wealth they created.

Sub Step 5—The government taxes the corporation and the workers.

Step 6—The workers and owners must save and invest and they do so by depositing currency into corporate ownership (stock) or corporate debt (bonds).

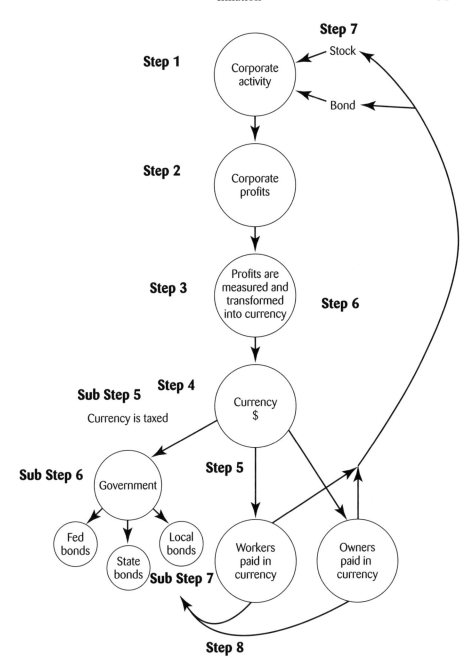

Sub Step 6–The government workers are paid from the taxes of corporate
profits. The government purchases goods and services with the tax revenue from corporate profits.

Step 7–The currency saved is invested into corporate activity as follows:

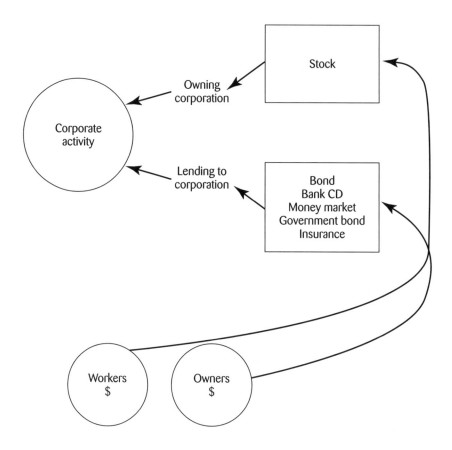

Sub Step 7–The government spends more money than it was able to tax
away from corporate profits and must borrow additional money from
the workers and owners. Government bonds are necessary to pay off government debt.

Step 8–Workers or owners could invest in government bonds.

The problem with inflation is between Steps 2 and 5. The printing of
the currency is supposed to match the amount of actual production.

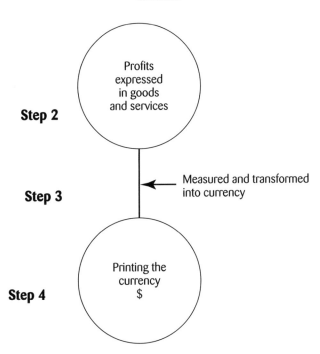

The currency can be artificially expanded or contracted by a variety of methods. This expansion or contraction of Step 4 means the currency is no longer matched in value relative to production.

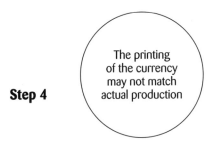

By lowering interest rates, taxes or utilities, the currency is expanded.

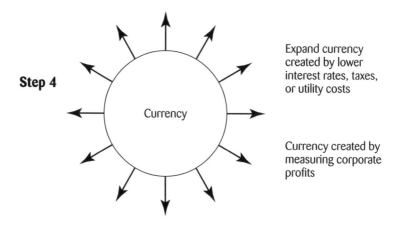

Step 4

Currency

Expand currency
created by lower
interest rates, taxes,
or utility costs

Currency created by
measuring corporate
profits

The result of the expanded currency is more money for everyone. However, the expanded currency is not real. The value of currency cannot be increased in reality because the currency represents a real piece of steel, a real piece of finished product, a real productive thought, and so on.

Expanding the currency is inflationary. It means as the currency is artificially expanded (more currency printed which is not justified by corporate production) the value of the currency actually shrinks. If the currency is artificially expanded by 10 percent then the shovel in the hardware store which costs $10 will, as a result of the expanded currency, cost $11. That is, it now takes 10 percent more money to buy the same item because the currency was expanded by 10 percent.

Why would the government attempt to expand the currency? The objective is to improve a slumping economy. The economy takes years to either expand or contract. The economy is stimulated into expansion by increasing corporate activity. To increase corporate activity, corporations need more money. By temporarily creating more currency, the corporations will receive the additional money through both investment and purchase of goods and services. The expansion of the currency will not actually show up in the change in prices for several years. Therefore, if the currency is expanded today, the price of the shovel might not go up for three to four years in the future. By then, it is hoped, the expansion of the currency will have had a positive effect on corporate activity—expanding corporate activity—expanding corporate profits so that the expanded corporate profits catch up with the expanded currency.

As an example, assume it takes four years to expand the economy. The first year of the expansion begins with the government increasing the supply of currency beyond what is justified through production, the second and third years of the stimulation, the corporations which create the wealth improve their ability to produce because there is more money in the economy. By the fourth year the corporation actually begins to increase the amount of corporate profits above the rate of profits before the stimulation occurred.

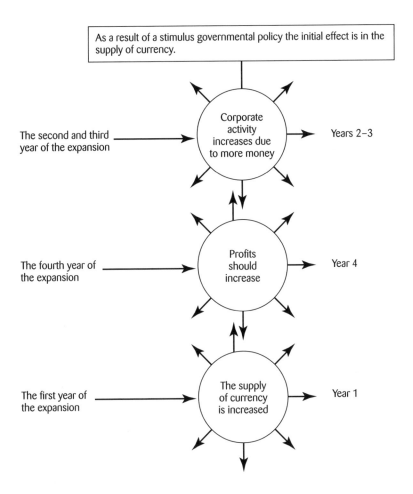

Then the expanded currency finds its way back to corporate activity and the greater corporate activity generates more corporate profit. More corporate profit makes everyone more wealthy.

The wealth of society can only be increased by increasing corporate profits.

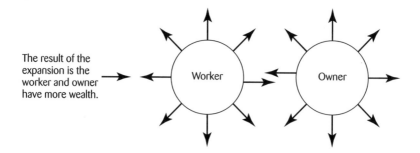

The result of the expansion is the worker and owner have more wealth.

Inflation can damage an economy when the expansion of the currency outpaces the long-term growth grate of corporate profits. The most dramatic effect of currency expansions is observed during wartime. Economics are temporarily put aside and money for war supplies is printed in abundance. This rapid overprinting creates an inflation upspike associated with a significant conflict. The following graph illustrates the inflation upsurge of the War of 1812, Civil War, World War I, World War II, and the Vietnam War.

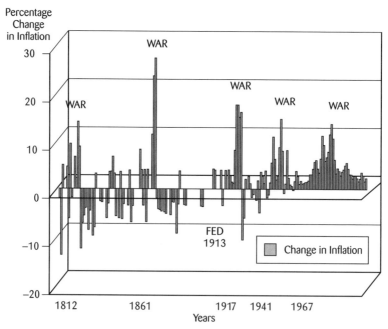

Inflation During the Wars

Source: U.S. Department of Labor.

Inflation is the lowering of the value of the currency. It occurs when the relative relationship between the actual goods and services produced is outpaced by the growth of currency. Currency should grow at the exact rate of corporate profits to be at zero inflation. When currency grows too fast or faster than production, inflation results.

Deflation is caused by shrinking the currency.

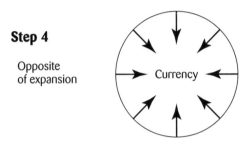

Step 4

Opposite of expansion

Decreased currency created by high interest rates, high taxes or high utilities

Currency is created by measuring corporate profits

Currency is reduced by increasing interest rates, taxes, or utility costs. The currency is always being either expanded (stimulated) or reduced (constricted) depending upon the current economic condition. However, deflation is more difficult to create because a modern society has moved from actually using cash to make a transaction, to using electronic money which is produced from credit cards.

Constrictive governmental policy cannot stop the use of a credit card. The depression of the 1870s and the 1930s was essentially caused by aggressive governmental reduction in available currency. Currency was simply taken out of the economy, thus collapsing it. Today, a citizen can make a purchase without currency. A ten-dollar shovel can be purchased with a credit card even if no currency is available.

Regardless, when inflation begins to show up in the price of goods and services, the currency supply will be reduced by higher interest rates, higher taxes, or higher utilities. It then will take several years for the reduction in currency to reduce corporate profits.

Inflation is caused by tampering with Step 4. The government has the power to increase or decrease the amount of currency regardless of corporate profits actually generated in terms of wealth creation. The creation of currency should match actual production, but it typically does not. Typically, currency is overprinted, creating ongoing inflation.

Overprinting of currency causes the need to use more currency to buy a product from year to year. It causes price increases not due to the product changing price, but due to the currency decreasing in value. If $1200 was buried in 1970 and dug up in 2003 and the $1200 was taken to a Volkswagon dealer to purchase a new VW Bug, the dealer would reject the $1200 as insufficient. In 1970 the price of a new VW Bug was $1200. By 2003 the price of a similar automobile was $20,000. The value of the automobile is essentially the same. It is the currency that has changed value. A dollar of the old currency is only worth $0.10 to $0.15 because the government overprinted the currency year in and year out. Businesses cannot cause inflation, consumer spending habits cannot cause inflation, wars cannot cause inflation; the only cause of inflation is more currency being created then there is production to justify.

Government allows the overcreation of currency for several reasons, some justifiable and some less than honorable. A shortage of currency is a disaster. Too little money in circulation will collapse business. Printing a perfect match between the amount of currency and amount of production would create zero inflation but it also would make it difficult to establish business growth. There must be money available to implement business inventions, creations, and expansions. If a cure for cancer is created there must be currency available now to build the cancer cure factory. Such currency that exists in the present to be used to implement production in the future would have had to have been overprinted currency. It is to the benefit of society in general to have available currency to implement inventiveness and/or improvements. Nevertheless, the overprinting causes some inflation regardless of the benefits. In other words, the down side to the benefit of available currency is some inflation. Elected government representatives are surely tempted to overprint currency to buy votes. The government budget, when it exceeds revenue, causes the overprinting of currency, which causes some inflation.

During a business down cycle, currency can be created by lowering interest rates and lowering taxes. All currency must eventually find its way back to corporate activity. By expanding the supply of currency, production will eventually be expanded. Although this accepted method to improve general economic conditions by improving production works quite well, it is also inflationary. The nature of the measurement economic system has a necessary residue of inflation. Inflation can never go to zero and it can never go negative: it is always positive in a modern society.

The long-term investor must understand that every rate of return is pulled slightly backward by inflation. A rate of return that is too low can be brought to a negative rate (loss) by the power of inflation.

Inflation is like the constant current of a large river. If the river has an average three-knot current and the boater buys an outboard engine to power a canoe when the engine is only capable of producing forward movements of two knots, then the canoe is incapable of making forward progress against the current. An investor's net return must exceed inflation to actually make a gain.

Supply and Demand

Corporate profits in aggregate grow at a long-term, steady, positive rate. This long-term, steady growth rate is very predictable on a ten-year average basis. As time decreases from ten years down to a five, the behavior becomes less predictable and for periods of less than five years there is virtually no predictability.

Short-term supply and demand changes can cause a rapid fluctuation in the price of any security or commodity. Investors often place too much importance on rapid, short-term price changes. Assumptions are made and incorrect logical leaps are established by investors who falsely conclude a supply and demand change is a long-term situation. Investors assume a supply and demand event will be a long-term norm and invest accordingly, only to be disappointed when the effects of supply and demand dissipate. As the short-term effects of supply and demand dissipate back to normal conditions, the average growth rate of corporate profits will prevail in all markets.

Every investor must have a basic understanding of how supply and demand affect prices. Imagine attending a wedding in the middle of the summer in Arizona on top of a plateau. The top of the plateau is only accessible by helicopter because the upper surface where the wedding is being held is approximately the size of a football field with a sheer thousand-foot drop on all sides. During the wedding, news arrives that all flight activity will be cancelled for the next three days. A hundred wedding guests formally dressed, in 100 degree heat, who were expecting to depart in only a few hours must now remain exposed to the harsh elements for seventy-two hours.

During the wedding, prior to the flight cancellation, drinks were provided at cost; $5 per drink to cover the cost of transportation and distribution. Without realizing the economic environment on top of the plateau has changed since the news of the flight cancellation, several of the guests approach the bartender and ask for a glass of cold, refreshing water. The bartender smiles and says, "That will be fifty dollars." Outraged, the guests protest and the bartender agrees the price of the water does not properly reflect the situation and promptly puts up a sign, "Water, $1000 per glass.

Pay or go thirsty." Pundits speculate the price could go up to $50,000 and offer the bartender $10,000 for one hundred glasses of water.

The price of water rapidly increased because the demand (consumption needs of the wedding guests) increased above what was expected, due to the cancellation of the helicopter flight. The water supply was insufficient to meet the needs of one hundred wedding guests for seventy-two hours, as the wedding was originally expected to last only four hours.

A rainstorm poured on the plateau the first evening and continued for the next fifty hours. When the heavy rain started, the price of the water decreased because no one needed water from the bartender. Guests simply held up their glasses and Mother Nature did the rest. The price of water dropped to zero on the wedding plateau.

Before the Iraqi war, a similar supply and demand question evolved over the price of oil. Iraq, which had a large supply of oil, was not selling the oil due to a decade-long embargo. As a consequence, many of its oil wells' pumping mechanisms were in disrepair, further driving production down.

Due to a bizarre quirk in global politics, the impending war was clearly telegraphed months in advance. Everyone knew the war was coming and it would not start for several months. It was to the advantage of political party A to have the price of oil decline and the opposite was true for political party B.

The price of oil increased and political party B told anyone who would listen the price of oil would go up as a result of a war in Iraq. Party B cited the rising price as a foreshadowing of future events and said once the war started the price would go up more. Political party B would gain votes if people believed the price of oil would increase. Political party B misstated what would happen to the price of oil because the price of oil under such circumstances is a basic supply and demand question identical to the situation on the Arizona plateau.

Shortly before the Iraqi war, oil companies stopped buying oil because they knew once the war started the price would decline sharply. Why should a refiner pay $40 per barrel when shortly into the future the price would likely be $25? Short-term supplies were limited and the short-term prices increased. Pundits speculated the price of oil would increase further, which drove up the short-term price even further. Clearly, when Iraq was attacked, the embargo would be lifted and Iraq would have to sell oil on the world market at a high rate to obtain money to rebuild. Iraq would rain oil on the world market, increasing the world supply, driving the price down—sharply down—just as the rain on the plateau dropped the price of water. Political party B also lied and said the American oil companies wanted to attack Iraq because they are _____ (you fill in the blank—*mean, greedy* etc.) However, political party B wanted to take advantage of the situation to promote the concept of domestic corporations' war mongering tendencies to gain votes. Oil companies want the price of oil to be high, not low. Oil companies make more money when the price of oil is high, not low. Attacking Iraq dropped the price of oil 40 percent, which means the corporate profits of all the U.S. oil companies dropped 40 percent. That is bad news for American oil, not good news. Political party B used the situation not to inform the public, but to gain political advantage. In addition, these price changes could take many years to settle into normal market conditions.

Investors must realize political parties will saturate the public airwaves with untruths to gain political advantage. The investor cannot use such information for the purpose of making sound investment decisions.

Supply and demand can cause short-term price changes. Speculative investor behavior during a rapid change in market price is a dangerous game. There is an old economic adage, "A pine tree can't grow to the moon." At some point, pine trees stop growing, die, and fall over. It is cheaper to substitute methanol as a replacement for gasoline when the price per barrel of oil exceeds $50. Like the pine tree, the price per barrel of oil can only go so high before it stops growing. If methanol were mass-produced it would be even cheaper. The price of oil can only go so high before it is substituted with another commodity. History is full of speculators who said the price of x would go to some extraordinary height.

The speculators are always incorrect because all wealth is derived from corporate activity and the resulting profits. Rapid short-term price changes due to a particular temporary supply and demand phenomenon is a difficult environment for the average investor—particularly the pension investor—to take advantage of. Rapid price changes are temporary, exacerbated by politics, and compounded by speculation. Eventually short-term price pressure dissipates and markets return to normal. Corporate profits grow at a steady rate and nothing can change that. The economy grows at the rate of population growth plus productivity.

Real World
Investment Choices

There is only one place to invest currency in a profit sharing and/or 401(k) plan. There is only one place to invest. All wealth is created by corporate profits; therefore the only investment opportunity is to invest in corporate activity.

Corporate activity can be purchased under a varying set of expected risk and expected rate of return scenarios. The investor can specify how much volatility and how much return is desired.

The typical employee, self-directed, profit sharing and/or 401(k) plan offers approximately twelve investment choices. Each investment option is a vehicle to deposit currency into corporate activity at varying predetermined levels of expected risk (volatility) and return. The investor decides what rate of return is necessary to meet his individual retirement needs, being mindful that all rates of return have associated levels of risk.

The following table describes the twelve typical investment choices in a profit sharing and 401(k) plan.

Name of Choice	What It Is Invested In	Expected Return	Expected Zigzag Rate (or standard deviation)	Time to Recover
Money Market (mutual fund)	Very short-term corporate IOUs. Typically 30 to 120 days, 1 year maximum.	Lowest possible return called the risk-free rate of return (e.g. 3%)	0	0 Years
Short-Term Corporate Bonds (mutual fund)	Corporate bonds (IOUs) from 1 to 3 years in maturity.	4%	5%	2 Years

Name of Choice	What It Is Invested In	Expected Return	Expected Zigzag Rate (or standard deviation)	Time to Recover
Corporate or Government Bonds (mutual fund)	Corporate IOUs (bonds) with maturity dates 15 years or less.	5.5%	8%	5 Years
Stocks in Real Estate Properties (mutual fund)	Corporate ownership in rental property, typically commercial.	9%	15%	10 Years
Large Cap Stock (big companies) Dividend Fund (mutual fund)	Corporate ownership of large companies which pays an above average dividend.	9.5%	17%	10 Years
Large Cap Stock (typically the top 500 U.S. corporations) (mutual fund)	Corporate ownership in some or all of the top 500 U.S. corporations.	11%	20%	10 Years
Stock Mid-Cap (mutual fund)	Corporate ownership in U.S. corporations smaller than the largest 500 corporations but larger than the 1000 smallest.	13%	25%	10 Years
Global Stock (mutual fund)	Corporate ownership in both domestic corporations and non-U.S. corporations.	14%	27%	12 Years
Non-U.S./ Foreign Stock (mutual fund)	Corporate ownership in non-U.S. corporations.	15%	30%	10–15 Years

Name of Choice	What It Is Invested In	Expected Return	Expected Zigzag Rate (or standard deviation)	Time to Recover
Small Cap Stock (mutual fund)	Corporate ownership in corporations smaller than the top 1000 to 1500 U.S. corporations.	16%	34%	15–20 Years
Small Aggressive Growth Companies' Stock (mutual fund)	Corporate ownership in small, fast growing corporations— often globally.	18%	40%	15–20 Years
The Employer's Company Stock (mutual fund)	Corporate ownership in employers' stock.	?	100%	Maybe Never

The following is a brief explanation of each investment choice.

1. A money market fund is characterized by zero volatility and the lowest rate of return in the financial markets. Currency is loaned to corporations on a very short-term basis (30 to 120 days), essentially very short-term corporate bonds or corporate lending. It is the shortness of the lending that creates the illusion of zero volatility. There is technically some volatility but it is hidden by the manager of the money market fund.

$$\frac{\$2000 \text{ per year for 40 years} \quad \dfrac{1\% \text{ growth rate}}{\text{zero zigzag}}}{} = \text{expected future value of } \$99,000$$

years to recover from down market = 0
return   = low
volatility   = 0
risk—When inflation and taxes are subtracted from money market returns there is typically a loss of principal. If new car prices grow at 5% then a 1% growth rate in a savings rate account will fall behind car prices.

2. An investment in short-term corporate bonds is the loan of currency to corporations with the payback of principal typically in around three years. The mutual fund manager is mostly invested in bonds with the average maturity date of three years. Some bonds will have maturities in less than three years and some bonds will be greater than three years. Most of the volatility (standard deviation) and the rate of return of bonds is determined by the maturity date. As maturity increases, volatility increases, and the rate of return normally increases (there are short-term periods where this is reversed). A twenty-five-year-old depositing $2000 per year into a 401(k) plan investing in short-term corporate bonds will experience the following:

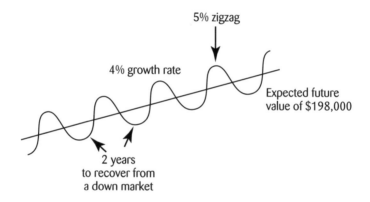

3. Corporate bonds are currency loaned to corporations with maturities of the loans/bonds as long as three to fifteen years. Assume assets are diversified in a mutual fund.

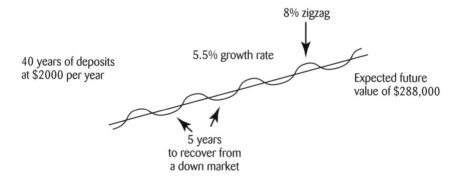

Numbers 4 through 12 are all 100 percent invested in various forms of corporate ownership (stock).

4. Real Estate stock funds buy stock, corporate ownership in businesses that typically buy some type of commercial rental property, or speculate in commercial real estate price changes. Assume mutual fund.

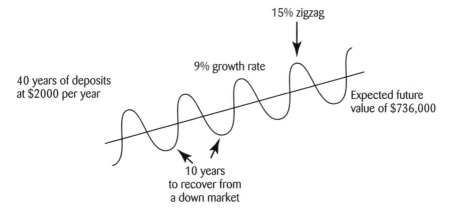

15% zigzag

9% growth rate

40 years of deposits
at $2000 per year

Expected future
value of $736,000

10 years
to recover from
a down market

5. Fortune 500 corporations which pay the owners (stockholders) a dividend. Assets are 100 percent invested in corporate activity of large corporations. Assume mutual fund.

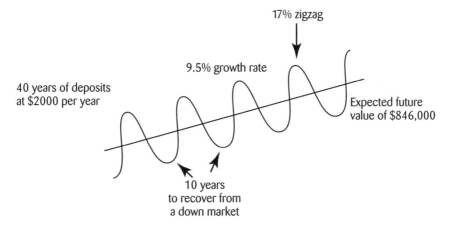

17% zigzag

9.5% growth rate

40 years of deposits
at $2000 per year

Expected future
value of $846,000

10 years
to recover from
a down market

6. Ownership in large domestic corporations, typically within the top 500 companies commonly referred to as large cap stocks. Assume mutual fund.

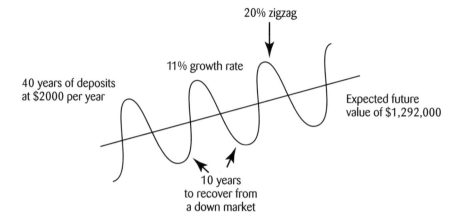

7. Corporate ownership in midsize domestic corporations, smaller than the largest 500, larger than the smallest 1000, commonly referred to as mid cap stocks. Assume mutual fund.

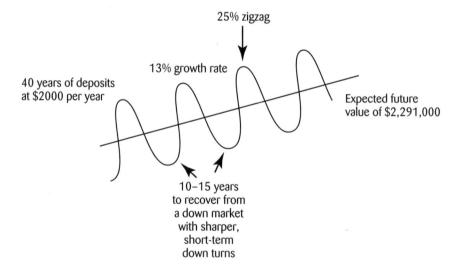

8. With global stocks, 100 percent of assets are invested in corporate activity. Global stock funds are a mixture of domestic and non-U.S. corporations. Typically larger corporations, these funds can also be made up of a mixture of larger, midsized, and small corporations. Assume mutual fund.

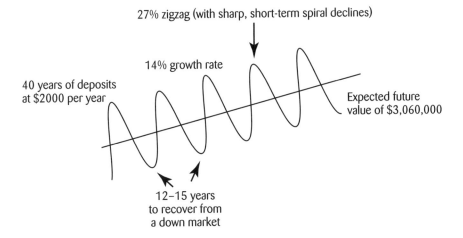

27% zigzag (with sharp, short-term spiral declines)

14% growth rate

40 years of deposits
at $2000 per year

Expected future
value of $3,060,000

12–15 years
to recover from
a down market

9. With foreign stocks, 100 percent of assets are invested in corporate activity. These stocks offer corporate ownership in non-U.S. corporations, typically larger corporations, but can also be a mixture of large, midsized, and small corporations. Assume mutual fund.

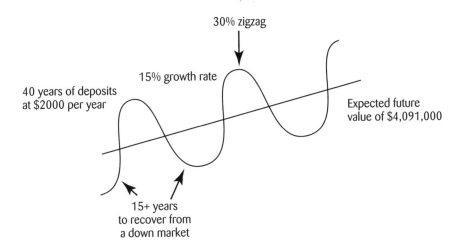

30% zigzag

15% growth rate

40 years of deposits
at $2000 per year

Expected future
value of $4,091,000

15+ years
to recover from
a down market

10. With small cap stocks, 100 percent of assets are invested in corporate activity. These stocks offer corporate ownership in companies smaller than the top 1000 to 1500. Assume mutual fund.

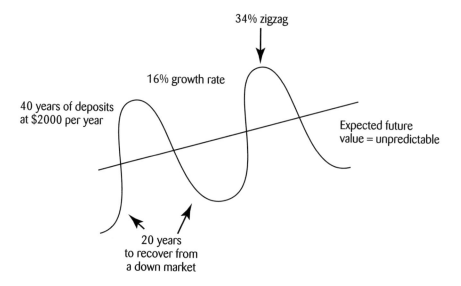

11. With an investment in small aggressive growth companies' stocks, 100 percent of assets are invested in corporate ownership. The definition of small aggressive stock is inconsistent. These stocks are typically global in nature. Assume mutual fund.

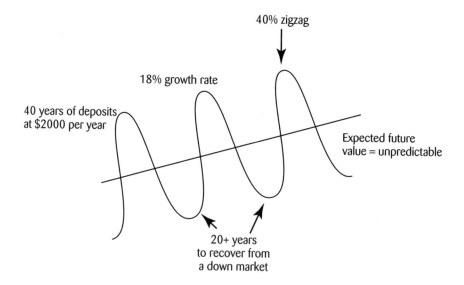

12. Some GE workers retire multi-millionaires, while Enron workers retire with zero. Assets when invested in a single stock can have the potential to suffer a 100 percent loss.

100% zigzag

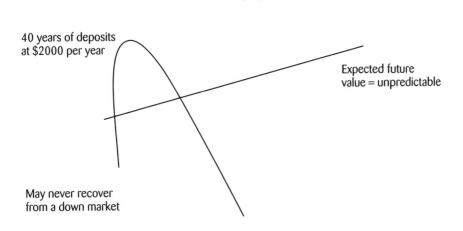

40 years of deposits
at $2000 per year

Expected future
value = unpredictable

May never recover
from a down market

Most 401(k) and profit sharing plans offer plan participants mutual funds as investment choices. Mutual funds are invested in 50 to 150 different stocks or bonds depending upon the investment objective of the mutual fund. No single mutual fund is diversified in terms of minimizing risk and maximizing returns. Only a mixture of funds in various markets can meet the definition of efficiency (minimized risk and maximized return).

It is necessary to mix the different funds to obtain the best possible rate of return at the lowest risk.

The following graph illustrates mixing mutual funds/markets to minimize volatility and maximize return potential.[21]

[21]Markowitz, Harry M. 1959 *Portfolio Selection: Efficient Diversification of Investments.* New York: John Wiley and Sons; Sharp, William F. 1964 "Capital Asset Price: A Theory of Market Equilibrium Under Conditions of Risk." *Journal of Finance* vol xix; Sharp, William F. 1970 *Portfolio Theory and Capital Markets.* New York: McGraw Hill.

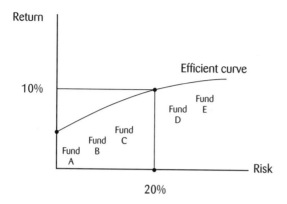

On the previous graph, Funds A, B, C, D, and E are all beneath the curve. An investor placing all of her assets in any single fund should experience an inefficient performance rate of return.

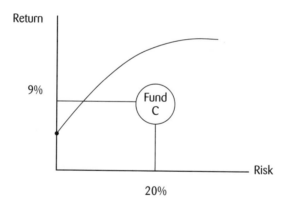

Fund C has a 20 percent volatility rate with a 9 percent rate of return. However, at a 20 percent level of volatility, the markets offer a higher return than Fund C at essentially the same risk. The curve illustrates the market potential at an efficient mixture of funds. Individually, Fund C is inferior to a mixture of funds. The bending curve is actually a representation of all possible mixes.

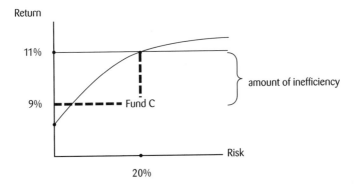

The only way to have an efficient portfolio is to be in multiple markets. The bending curve is representing all possible mixes: the curve is multiple markets and therefore is efficient.

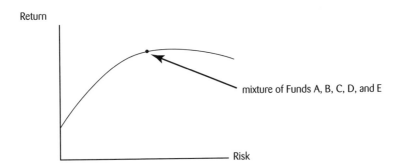

Every point on the efficiency curve represents a mixture of assets, not a single market or asset.

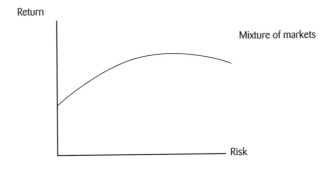

A 401(k) plan with investment choices in twelve different markets can enable the investor to construct an efficient mixture of funds at any expected rate of return and at any expected level of risk.[22]

Risk or volatility is washed away in time. Why would a twenty-five-year-old who intends to work for the next forty years be concerned about being invested in a market or mix of markets which has a potential ten-year down cycle? A ten-year down cycle cannot damage a forty-year target. If the long-term rate of return from a given market is high then the investor is significantly better off in high-paying, volatile investments rather than the low-rate-of-return, risk-free investment.

The investor does not need to be concerned with the short term loss of principal due to normal volatility until such time as the sale of securities is necessary to meet daily expenses. An investor at age twenty-five can weather a ten-year down cycle to earn a higher rate of return where a sixty-two-year-old close to retirement should be in a mixture of low standard deviation markets with only a three- to four-year down cycle.

The following table lists possible efficient mixes of markets for different age groups assuming an age sixty-five retirement target.

Name of Choice	Age 20–30	Age 40	Age 50	Age 60
Money Market (mutual fund)	0%	0%	10%	30%
Short-Term Corporate Bonds (mutual fund)	5%	10%	20%	20%
Corporate or Government Bonds (mutual fund)	5%	10%	20%	20%
Stocks in Real Estate Properties (mutual fund)	10%	10%	10%	10%
Large Cap Stock (big companies) Divident Fund (mutual fund)	15%	10%	10%	10%
Large Cap Stock (typically the top 500 U.S. corporations) (mutual fund)	15%	10%	10%	10%
Stock Mid Cap (mutual fund)	10%	10%	5%	0%
Global Stock (mutual fund)	5%	5%	0%	0%
Non-U.S./Foreign Stock (mutual fund)	20%	20%	15%	0%
Small Cap Stock (mutual fund)	10%	10%	0%	0%

(continued)

---

[22]Markowitz, Harry M. 1959 *Portfolio Selection: Efficient Diversification of Investments.* New York: John Wiley & Sons; Sharp, William F. 1964 "Capital Asset Prices: A Theory of Market Equilibrium Under Condition of Risk." *Journal of Finance* Vol. XIX; Sharp, William F. 1970 *Portfolio Theory and Capital Markets.* New York: McGraw Hill.

Name of Choice	Age 20–30	Age 40	Age 50	Age 60
Small Aggressive Growth Companies' Stock (mutual fund)	5%	5%	0%	0%
The Employer's Company Stock (mutual fund)	0%	0%	0%	0%

*The long term of corporate ownership is 2x bonds. As the future is unknown, the relative return of stocks is 2x bonds.

The twenty- or thirty-year-old investor can seek a higher rate of return because he is young enough to work through a lengthy down cycle. As the investor ages and moves closer to retirement there is progressively less time to work through the inevitable market fluctuations. By mixing mutual funds at various levels of risk the investor can create less risky mixes as retirement comes closer. A sixty-year-old can create a portfolio with a short enough down cycle as to not affect the safety of principal.

There is a misguided fear of market cycles. Attempts to avoid down markets can destroy a long-term rate of return. The young need not fear a down market.

Down markets are opportunities for a 40-year-old and trouble for an over-invested 60-year-old. By analyzing the two bear markets of the twentieth century, the Great Depression which started in 1929 and ended in 1938, and the recession of the 1970s, which began in 1973 and ended in 1982, it is possible to see the benefits of long-term investments.[23]

An investor who had $10,000 in stock in 1929 essentially still had the $10,000 in value intact by 1938. Yes, the principal declined through the first four years of the Depression, but it recovered within ten years. Both large cap (big companies) and small cap (small companies) stocks experienced no growth through the Great Depression and no loss either. It is the "no loss" issue that is important because the Great Depression is the economic statistical worst case scenario. The statistical worst case scenario of the stock market is a ten-year down period where no loss of principle occurs if the investor remains invested for the entire ten years.

Investors in 401(k) and profit sharing plans have two investment issues. One is the change in value of their account balance and the other is the future value of the ongoing stream of deposits. Depositing money into stock from 1929 to 1938 was very profitable. Depositing $2000 per year for ten years throughout the Depression in small cap stocks created $20,000 in

---

[23]Ibbotson and Associates. *SBBI 2003 Yearbook Results for 1926–2002: Stock, Bonds, Bills, and Inflation.* Chicago: Ibbotson Associates.

principal plus $46,000 in gains for a total of $66,000. The average annualized rate of return was 24 percent. The rate of return for deposits is higher in down markets than in up markets.

The rate of return of $2000 invested in large cap stocks through the Great Depression was $20,000 in principal plus $16,700 in gains, equaling $36,700 in total with an average annualized rate of return of 12.9 percent. Why would a 40-year-old be concerned in 1929 about a stock market decline when the forty-year-old has twenty-five years more to work? A down market for a forty-year-old is good news because the future wealth of the forty-year-old will be determined by his future deposits, not whether his principal gained or moved sideways for only ten years. Down markets are good for the young. On the other hand, a sixty-three-year-old 100 percent invested in stock in 1929 would likely have to postpone retirement for another ten years. Being 100 percent invested in stocks when close to retirement when the investor must live off the assets in the 401(k) or profit sharing plan is an error. Being fully invested in a market with a ten year or greater potential down cycle when only two years from retirement can cause a financial failure. A ten-year decline is good for a twenty-, thirty-, forty-, or fifty-year-old, but bad for those fifty-five and older. The solution is simple: reduce the percentage of stock in the 401(k) portfolio as retirement approaches.

What Makes Us Richer and What Makes Us Poorer

There is only one source of wealth, the wealth created from corporate activity and its resulting profits. An investor on Planet Corn has only one strategy to build wealth. Planet Corn is a single commodity world and 100 percent of all goods and services are created by corn production. To become wealthy on Planet Corn, the investor must buy and own corn production. A young worker on Planet Corn is best served by obtaining corn producing land inch by inch until, over a lifetime, enough producing land has been acquired to generate enough income to live off of during retirement. Forget the dollar value of the land year to year; just steadily buy it.

Lending money to the corn farmer is not an optimal strategy because corn-producing land produces wealth at twice the return a lender receives. Lending money to the government of Planet Corn pays the investor at only half the rate of return the producing farm generates. The government on Planet Corn is only worth its share of corporate profits generated from the producing farm. If there was not any corn production then there would be no government.

In a modern society all wealth is derived from corporate activity and its resulting profits. Profits then define wealth. Profits are the production in excess of the internal needs of the producing corporation. Profits are produced in the form of goods and services and the goods and services are measured in a standardized unit. The standardized units must represent the goods or service they are measured from, making the standardized unit actually worth something.

The process by which profits expressed in goods and services are transformed to currency is called measurementism. Measurementism is simply measuring the profits and printing a corresponding amount of currency. During an educational meeting I was conducting, a steelworker said, "Capitalism is a conspiracy against the people." He did not understand measurementism is capitalism and what measurementism does is simply measure how much production occurred. Measurementism means measuring. If a windowsill is 24 inches wide and it is measured with a tape measure and found to be 24 inches wide, it is 24 inches because it is simply 24 inches wide.

A 24-inch wide windowsill is not a conspiracy against the people. Why would the people care if a windowsill is 24 inches wide or not?

Measurementism simply measures. Measurementism is not a conspiracy against the people. People would be irrational not to measure whatever it is that needs measuring. Measuring profits that are represented as goods and services so the profits can be exchanged into currency is the result of the simplest of rational thinking.

The act of measuring profits into currency is measurementism. The fancier name is capitalism. Capitalism means the dollar bill is actually some amount of real corporate activity; a little piece of steel, butter, wheat, plastic, or useful thinking. Capitalism makes the dollar really worth something so it can be exchanged for goods and services.

To make more money, profits must become greater. Any activity which makes profits greater makes us richer. Any activity which makes profits smaller makes us poorer.

All wealth is derived from corporate activity and its resulting profits. The more money put into corporate activity the richer we become; the less money returned to the source of wealth the poorer we become. If corporate profits were $100 what event would make us richer?

The highest possible wealth creation scenario:

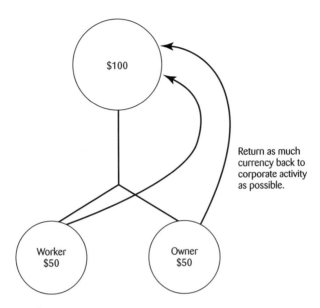

Due to taxes, corporate profits are reduced before the workers and owners are paid.

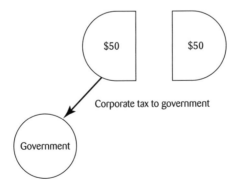

The remaining $50 is taxed as income tax where half goes to the government.

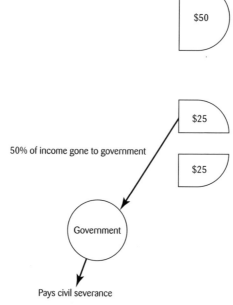

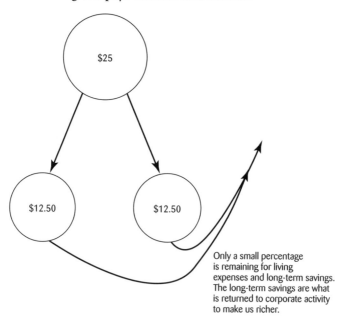

The remaining $25 pays workers and owners.

Returning all of the $100 in profit to corporations would make us the richest, but the corporate activity does not own all of the $100. The government takes 75 percent of it via corporate tax and income tax. Add sales tax and the earners of corporate profit only receive $0.20 on the dollar earned. This means if a farmer on Planet Corn produced a hundred pounds of wealth for himself, he is then worth a hundred pounds of corn. He is a hundred pounds rich. The government takes eighty pounds, now the farmer is only twenty pounds rich. Twenty pounds is less rich than a hundred pounds. Twenty thousand dollars is less rich than $100,000. If a worker has $20,000 then the worker is less well off then he would have been if he had $100,000.

The worker must save for the future and meet daily living expenses at retirement. The higher the savings rate, the richer the worker will become and vice versa. When taxes—either corporate taxes or income, sales, real estate, user, local, state, or regional add-on taxes—disable the worker to barely meet living expenses, then it creates a situation where the savings rate is either too low or nothing. When the population cannot afford to put money (a measured unit of corporate profits, also called capital because the money actually represents real value) into long-term savings the entire country becomes poorer.

The greater proportion of corporate profits received by those who earn the corporate profits, the richer each individual will become and the richer the country will become. Being richer provides the following:

Better medical care—very important when being operated on.
Better tanks—very important when at war.
Better education—very important to long-term wealth.
Better art—makes life nice.
Better religion—makes life nice.
Better housing—more people can own a home if corporate profits increase.
Fewer poor—the more profits the richer the average citizen—compare Boston to Calcutta.
Retirement is possible—years of life without work.
Higher life expectancy—in Russia the life expectancy is fifty-five while in the United States it is seventy-five. Maybe money does not buy happiness, but it does buy 20 years of extra life.
Better food—safest food supply.

More invention—the rate of discovery is directly related to the rate of
   growth of corporate profits.
More firefighters—firefighters are paid by corporate profits.
More police officers—police officers are paid by corporate profits.
Political freedom—economic freedom and political freedom are synonymous.
All jobs—all jobs are 100 percent paid for by corporate profits.
Better everything—all things are created by corporate activity and its re-
   sulting profits. The more profits, the better life is, the longer life is, and
   the happier life is.

Any event which reduces corporate profits makes life worse. The best
strategy maximizes profits.

In the hunting village, if there is a shortage of food, clothing, and shelter, the remedy is for the hunting party to produce more deer meat and deer
by-products which are used for 100 percent of all food, clothing, and shelter.

If the chief desires to build a big teepee, called the Convention Center
Teepee, it does not create more food, clothing, and shelter. The Convention
Center Teepee does not make the village richer.

If the chief allows gambling, the village does not receive additional
deer meat. Only the hunting party can provide more deer meat and deer by
products. If the chief allows the daughters and wives of the hunter to become prostitutes, it does not make the village richer.

If the village teacher needs more food and shelter to educate the villagers better, then only the hunting party becoming more productive can
accomplish and increase resources. Gambling, prostitution, a new stadium,
and convention centers do not make the village richer. A new steel mill, a
new assembly plant, mining, farming, or productive thinking makes the village richer.

The lower taxes are, the higher amount is returned to corporate activity. Taxes make us poorer because taxes reduce corporate activity.

The government suing a corporation makes us poorer. Some think it
is fun to attack a huge business such as Microsoft. It might be fun but it is
Microsoft who will pay the future social security recipient. It is Microsoft
who pays the teacher, police officer, firefighter, county clerk, and spiritual
leader. We might rethink attacking the only source of wealth which is corporate activity and its resulting profits.

The long-term investor has the choices explained on the following
pages. The correct answer is determined by the highest return.

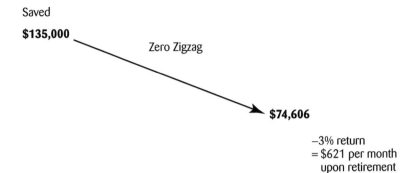

Saved

$135,000

Zero Zigzag

$74,606

−3% return
= $621 per month
upon retirement

$60,000 = $500 per month
Estimated monthly income is based on annuity
where $60,000 will generate $500 per month.

Saving Currency
Locking money in a strong box over a working lifetime saving $3000 per year for
45 years.

Saved

$135,000 ——————————— **$169,443**

+1% return
= $1,412 per month
upon retirement

100% of the monthly payment is paid by corporate profits.

Saving Under the Social Security System
Saving $3000 per year with Social Security
The risk-free return minus 75% = 1% rate of return

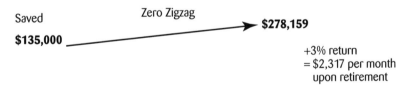

Saved

Zero Zigzag

$278,159

$135,000

+3% return
= $2,317 per month
upon retirement

100% of the monthly payment is paid by corporate profits.

Saving in a Money Market Fund or Buying 30- to 365-Day Corporate Debt IOUs

Saved   8% Zigzag Rate

$135,000   **$479,000**

+5% return
= $3,992 per month
upon retirement

100% of the principal investment are paid for by corporate profits.

Savings Deposited into Corporate Bonds or 10 Year Debt IOUs of Corporations

20% Zigzag Rate

Saved   **$2,959,915**

$135,000

+11% return
= $24,665 per month
upon retirement

100% of the principal interests are paid for by corporate profits.

Savings Deposited into Corporate Stocks
Buy Ownership in the Production Process

20% Zigzag Rate

$20,627,000

Saved

$135,000

+17% return
= $171,982 per month
upon retirement

100% of the principal interests are paid for by corporate profits.

Savings Deposited into Corporate Stocks (if there were no corporate taxes)
Buy Ownership in the Production Process

The table below illustrates the consequence of a lifetime of investment choices given $135,000 in savings. If an investor put $3,000 into a 401(k) and was 100 percent invested in stock, then the likely outcome is around $24,000 per month. Unfortunately the $171,000 per month is impossible because all corporations are taxed. The example of the $171,000 per month is to point out that taxes make us poorer, not richer.

Saving $3000 per year for 45 years will result in the following monthly payments.

	Investment Choice	Volatility	Monthly income
Figure 1	Saving currency	no zigzag	$621 per month
Figure 2	Social Security	no zigzag	$1,412 per month
Figure 3	Money market	no zigzag	$2,317 per month
Figure 4	Bonds	8% up or down	$3,992 per month
Figure 5	Large-Cap Stocks	20% up or down	$24,665 per month
Figure 6	Large Cap Stocks if no taxes were paid	20% up or down	$171,982 per month

The next time a presidential candidate tells you taxing the mean old greedy corporation is a good idea think about this: Your Social Security is going to pay you approximately $1,412 per month. If your assets were invested properly and there was zero corporate tax then you would have an amount similar to $171,000 per month. Think about it.

What is the safest strategy? Which investor will be safer? Is it more risky to live off of $1,400 per month or $24,000 per month? If the retiree becomes ill and the operation costs $100,000 the person with the $1,400 per month will die and the person with the $24,000 per month will live. The conclusion is, it is safer to have more money than less. Twenty-four thousand dollars is significantly more per month than $1,400.

Do taxes make us richer or poorer? A person with no taxes has $171,892 dollars per month. The Social Security system provides the average retiree with approximately $1,400 per month with the exact same input. Who is richer, a person with $1,400 per month or a person with $171,000 per month?

Of all the monthly income choices, corporations pay 100 percent of all the gains regardless of how the money is invested. The profits corporations generate are the only source of wealth. The more profits generated the better life will be for the citizen of the United States, world, Planet Corn, or the hunting village.

All wealth is generated by corporate profits. The investor is free to choose in what manner they want to receive corporate profits. Corporate profits are paid out in the value of the currency which government constantly lessens in value through inflation. Corporate profits can be paid in the form of interest payments to lenders, from the corporate IOUs (bonds). The bond buyer does not participate in the growth of the corporation. For the stock buyer corporate profits are paid as 100 percent of his share of the corporate profits.

The investor who wishes to accumulate as much wealth over her lifetime as possible should buy stock, which is corporate ownership. All other investment choices offer significantly less.

Pretendism

Pretendism is the opposite of measurementism. Under the pretendistic economic system government controls the value of the currency and the currency is not related to corporate profits. The citizen of a pretendistic system must pretend the money has value because it actually does not.

As long as everyone pretends the money has value the system works. The problem is, a pretend system is just that, a totally make-believe economic world. Though it is a very real world of whips, torture chambers, and prison. If an individual recognizes that the value of the currency is actually worthless (i.e. made up), then the individual is a threat to the pretend valuation and is then a threat to the pretend system. A person who becomes a threat to the system must be eliminated.

If someone stands up in a movie theater right before the climax of a partially engrossing science fiction film and screams "this giant bug movie is not real," the movie is ruined for everyone. A similar effect happens when a citizen of the pretendistic economy stands up and yells "this money is worthless." The individual must be incarcerated and either beaten to death or beaten sufficiently to force him to play along. Therefore, individual rights are impossible under pretendism. There are not any individuals in a pretendistic society and any attempts to step forward and be an individual will be met with all the force society can bring to bear to stop individual expressions.

If 10 percent of the population came to the realization the money is worthless and the value is simply made up by a few ruling elites, then 10 percent of the population would be mercilessly imprisoned and beaten into submission and/or murdered.

Pretendism is a state of mind and mind control is then the role of the government. The citizen will live or die on what they think.

Prague, Czechoslovakia

Prague, Czechoslovakia, 1977. On spring break from the United Nation study abroad Geneva, Switzerland program. In a bar in Prague.

"What do you think of having Russian soldiers in your country?" The index finger of the young Czech at the bar now invaded by naïve American students rises slowly to his lips. The international symbol for quiet. "Shhh." Then he whispers, "The walls have ears."

The cocky American smirk is replaced by the very real awareness that this place is not Kansas, it is not Oz either, it is some unknown hell that few in the West could even imagine. An instinctive glance over the shoulder and a return whisper, "What do you mean the walls have ears!"

The Czech points to the door and without words, the signal is, "American, if you want to talk politics then let's take it outside." Why does he want to go outside with me? Does he want to fight, talk, run, or arrest me? I go. Maybe not the brightest move, but I go anyway. Outside in the park I ask again, "What do you mean the walls have ears?" With a tone of, "You have to be kidding me," the impatient Czech gives another "Shhh!" Walking away from the trees he says, "The trees have ears." I just look forward as I walk, the mood to have a discussion is over, I want to run, far from here, a world where the American consulate is of no help, a place where the bars are bugged, the trees are bugged. A place where there are as many people listening from below the bar as there are people in the bar. There are as many people under me in the park listening as there are people in the park talking.

It became rapidly apparent that what was spoken could lead to a death sentence.

The Czech explains, "You cannot say what you think. Don't talk about the Russians, don't say anything other than 'May I have a beer, may I have a cigarette, or that female is pretty.' Because if you do, they will kill you." He continues, "What bothers us the most is they control what we think." I know what fear looks like. As a young college student, during a study abroad program, I learned what fear looks like.

Upon departing, I gave money to the Czech. Insulted, he refused it. I tried to explain to him why the money under pretendism is of no value in a world of measurementism. His money could not be exchanged back into any western currency. The financial system of Western Europe considered all the currency behind the Iron Curtain worthless. Because, in fact, Soviet currency was worthless in the most literal sense. It was a pretend currency. Its value was backed only by the power to kill anyone who disagreed about its purchasing power. As Soviet power stopped at the border, their currency also stopped at the border.

I had yet to go to business school, so my ability to explain exactly why the currency was worthless in the Western world was not very clear. Like most people, I did not understand money.

When the U.S.S.R. ended its false currency, the ruble was measured on the free markets and promptly collapsed into worthlessness. The ruble's true value was actually one fiftieth of what the ruling elite of the Soviet Union forced their people to accept. That is why the Iron Curtain money could not be exchanged into Western money. The ruble was not measured against the true production capabilities of the Soviet Union. The Communist party valued it at fifty times its true worth. Anyone behind the Iron Curtain who objected was eliminated.

The Czech said, "Let's buy beer with the money." He said he knew Czech beer tasted equally good on either side of the border. I agreed.

I witnessed the fall of pretendism on the evening news in 1989. I especially remember the street fighting in Prague. I saw a middle-aged man in a business suit lying in the street firing an automatic hand gun at the army. An automatic handgun has almost no combat usefulness against a well-armed militia. Yet there this civilian was, lying in the street firing a handgun at tanks. The cameraman was close enough to pick up the expression on his face. He was firing his handgun, aiming steadily, not shooting wildly but deliberately spacing his shots to optimize accuracy. There was no fear in his face, just total concentration and determination as he fired each shot. When an automatic pistol is fired the slide locks in the back position once the ammunition is expended. This civilian in a business suit fired his pistol and did not stop firing until the slide locked back. When he was out of ammo he ran for cover. While retreating, a young adolescent with an automatic rifle ran forward to provide covering fire.

My son asked why they were fighting. I said because the walls have ears and the people are tired of it.

Pretendism is an economic system where a few elite rulers are at the top and subjugate 90 percent of the population by creating money which has no relationship to production. When the money is untied from business activity then political power is concentrated among the few elites at the top. Any state of human consciousness objecting to the worthless currency is met by swift and merciless punishment, beatings, and death.

Why bring up pretendism in a book on managing pension assets? During my many years educating corporate employers on how to manage their 401(k) and profit sharing plan, occasionally—perhaps too often—someone will tell me he thinks measurementism is a bad idea and pretendism would be preferable to measurementism. Measurementism is dependent upon individual initiative, creativity, and the natural need to fulfill the dreams to produce. Maximizing production is best accomplished by maximizing humanity. Measurementism seeks a natural state of efficient production and therefore maximizes the human state of prosperity and achievement.

Pretendism cannot exist simultaneously with any individualized human thought. To think a thought under pretendism is a serious crime. I do not believe people truly understand what pretendism is or I doubt they would desire it.

Index